AS THE SUN RISES, IT DAWNS ON HIM

BY:

ROSS PATTERSON

DEDICATION

To the woman who got up and turned on a Shania Twain cd
immediately after we boned in Nashville circa 1994,
that don't impress me much.
Also, if I were you, I'd reconsider making dudes
whiskey sours and then explaining how it's your
"signature cocktail" after sex.
They tasted like shit.

CONTENTS

THE LIFE OF ST. JAMES ST. JAMES

June 11, 2015 McSorley's Old Ale House. New York, NY.

I take the last sip of my beer and pound the empty mug on the table next to my Remington Rand typewriter, before pulling out the last page of my second set of memoirs *When Darkness Falls, He Doesn't Catch It*. It's time to write my third, which you are reading right now. If you've come this far, chances are that you haven't had a dick in your ass and you've been in at least five fistfights in your life. Good for you. I don't even care if you're a homosexual male, just obviously be on top. It shows dominance... *which I will discuss in great detail later on*. Hopefully you didn't skip this foreword, or what you read will be a real fucking shock when you get to that chapter.

A heavyset Irish bartender in his mid 50's, Mickey, approaches. "Another one Saint James?"

"Yes please. These are going down way too easy."

"Well, you've also done a shit ton of cocaine."

I laugh. "Indeed I have. You know, I was here the night John McSorley died right up there," I say as I point to the flat above me.

"Is that so?"

"1910. I'll never forget that night. The traveling circus was in town and I banged out this beautiful contortionist from Romania while the Dog Faced Boy watched. I broke my hand punching their elephant in the rib cage that night."

Mickey looks at me confused. "I'm sorry, was John with you during this or—

"No. He was 83 years old and he died in his sleep. It was just a really great fucking night for me personally. Anywho, how about that beer?"

Mickey walks back behind the bar as I insert another blank piece of paper into the typewriter that Hemingway gave me. The fifty years I lived in New York City were some of the best times of my life. I was rich, we had electricity, and I was finally able to shit *inside* which was nice.

A lot of people say "fire" is the most important invention in human history, but those dickholes are wrong. Being able to drop a deuce ten feet away from your living room after a fresh cup of joe and enjoy indoor plumbing—to me—there's nothing like it. I always hated hobbling out into the snow and shitting on top of where 70 other grown men had already dumped out that day. In my eyes, Isaiah Rogers[1] is the real hero. Those cavemen can go fuck themselves.

The book you're about to read today is all about my time in New York City from 1869 through the 1940's. Cocaine was prescribed from a doctor still, it was fresh, and no one

---

1   *Isaiah Rogers invented indoor plumbing you fucking dummies. I knew I had to make this a footnote for you idiots.

was stepping on that shit yet. The girls were hot and desperate, pouring into Ellis Island every other day like hobos out of the last train car. The Stock Market was roaring and I was richer that a tit dipped in milk chocolate.

This is ultimately why I chose to write my memoirs here. You needed hubris and a set of brass to live here. If the streets caught you slipping, you fucking fell hard. Like most prosperous periods in my life, there was always a low point. That's the shit that hardens you like a Harvey Weinstein needle to the dick from an assistant in 98' on the eve of Sundance. You need that shot once in awhile to keep you going. If your life was all triumph, you could never regain that high and shit would be boring. No one wants to go through tough times right now in 2015, and it's only going to get worse I fear—hence why I'm leaving these memoirs behind.

You know the rules from the first two books, this will come to an end for me eventually. My pistol is still next me and I'm going to squeeze one off at the end of this shit. I'm not sure what year you are reading these books in right now, but I'm obviously dead as fuck in whatever decade you're currently living in. A quick Google search will tell you I didn't make it out of this week in June 2015. Hell, I wouldn't be surprised if my memoirs were banned from Amazon one day. The pussification of society is slowly creeping into every facet of life and you'll probably have to buy these books off the black market in the future.

However, you got a hold of them, just know that I was the last real man slinging my piss stick outside my pants wherever I please, and these patent white leather boots I'm wearing were made for fucking. Go ahead and throw a sock on the door knob and let people know you're enjoying my life. They'll also need something to strangle bate with later. You're welks.

Sincerely,

St. James St. James

Chapter 1

THE SECOND WORST
DAY EVER

January 15th, 1919 New York City

For ten minutes I stare at a mediocre painting called "The Family" by Egon Schiele hanging on the wall in my bathroom, when it suddenly dawns on me that I've been getting my dick sucked this entire time. I should probably rope off I think to myself as I look down and see an eager flapper girl[2] politely looking up at me. Obviously, I'm a gentleman, so I turn on the lights and make eye contact with her before depositing 14 ounces of semen into her mouth.

"You can go," I say as I wiggle my index and middle finger back and forth indicating for her to walk the fuck out of here.

After she exits, I towel off my dong with the precision of a Mexican's hands to the hood of Mustang at the end of a carwash, before zipping my pants up. I smile as I look at

---

2   *A "flapper girl" was a classier name for a whore in the 1920's. In their defense, they dressed nicer, but a whore is still a whore. You know it and I know it.

myself in the mirror. Goddamnit, I'm handsome as fuck and slicker a greased pig's asshole. With a comb made out of fox teeth, I adjust the part down the center of my hair, then pat down my pencil thin mustache with only my pinkies. Perfection.

I put my hand inside my coat pocket and pull out a baggie full of cocaine and dump a ridiculous amount out on my 24 carat gold bathroom sink. Yayo time, son. I pound down a gator tail of booger sugar like I've doing it for years… *probably because I have been doing it for years.* Get fucked brother, you know me at this point. This ain't the Himalayas, but I've been riding that yak as far back as when I moved here in 1869.

I know what you're thinking, "Saint James Street James, President Taft signed the Harrison Act in 1914 to prevent the sale of cocaine to the common man, how do you still have it?" I'm not the common man, motherfucker. I'm more powerful than Zeus's dick and I'm living that Gatsby life in NYC, baby.

The last fifty years have been kind to Daddy. I've invested in the market well and haven't bothered to get remarried. No need for that bullshit with this kind of night life. With indoor plumbing and electricity popping off for the last thirty years, there was no need to snuggle up to the same piece of ass for more than a day or so. It's not like the candles were going to blow out and we'd all be fucking cold again.

Was I pulling out every night? Fuck no. This city is littered with my seed. I probably pass a kid once a week on the streets who's carrying my genes. I always tip my cap and keep walking though. Put a picture on your wall of Honus Wagner if you're pining for someone to look up to. It ain't me. I got no time for anything other than whoring, drugs, and making the almighty dollar, chief.

I had a dope ass Model T that would have made Jerry Seinfeld cream his fucking jeans over, a sick brownstone in Greenwich Village, and a bar around the corner in which I'm still currently writing these memoirs in to this very day. No women allowed either, just the way God intended—if you believe in that bullshit. Whatever gets you through the day without strangle bating to death, so be it *holmes*. We're all just a geisha outfit, some white makeup, and two inches off the ground from making the wrong mistake, aren't we? RIP Carradine.

Once I give the other nostril a whiff of the ole' *bandito blanco*, I make my way downstairs to a full on fucking rager complete with an all black jazz band. Before you pull out a step stool to climb on your fucking high horse regarding race, black people play the best jazz on the planet. That's just a fact, Jack. Kenny G can take every last single inch of my cock into his mouth if he ever spouts off that he could do it better. White people are shit at jazz. I don't know when as a society we couldn't admit that certain races do shit better than other races, but I'll be goddamned at this stage of my life if you ever hear me say the words, "We are all created equal." Fuck no we aren't. Admit it and move on with your fucking life.

The party stops and stares as I walk down the steps like Danny fucking Kaye. There is an easiness about me that would make someone with Down Syndrome blush. Women clutch their pearls, one of them even slapped their own tiddy in awe. I point to the gold statue of Totally Fucking Mexico in the foyer, which I had shipped cross country and converted into a fountain. Obviously, the arm is still missing from where I pounded it into the ground to complete the Transcontinental Railroad in 1869. I thought about attaching a fake one, but it seemed tacky.

As my toes finally touch down on the 167th and final step, I smile as I move through the crowd greeting people as if I'm Mayor McCheese. You know damn well I slide my hand underneath some strange chick's dress then drop two digits under my nose after testing the merch. I wink at her husband, letting him know the grass is fresh and it's A-Okay to play croquet. My fingers tingle as I take a seat at the piano on the makeshift stage now vacated—after I punch the piano player in the face. I nod at the other musicians letting them know I'm about to tickle the ivories.

"Two, three, four," I say acknowledging a Latino man named "Juan" letting him know I didn't mean to leave him out.

The jazz musicians fall in line and smile, knowing full well I'm about to take them on a musical journey through life. What a fucking time to be alive. Everyone cheers and throws down drinks as they dance their dicks off. Through the window I can see the moon raising a full martini to me around minute twenty-three of a completely improvised jazz sesh. We were getting Thomas Edison lit up in this bitch, same as every other night before for the last ten years. Yeah, ten fucking years we were going this hard, and no—I didn't go to World War I.

The first World War was for poor people, or assholes who still had something to prove to their fathers. If you were cutting off the heads of chickens in a barn in Tiffin, Ohio during 1912, yeah, you were amped to go to war. For a big swinging dick like myself, there wasn't a goddamn prayer I was going to dig a ditch and freeze my midget fist off to shoot average weapons. Fuck that. Getting my dick sucked on the reg by hot ass immigrants who were rolling in by boat day after day suited me just fine.

People really discredit how the European immigrants really upped the sex factor up in this bitch. There were absolute dime pieces stepping off of barges daily who were one clean shower and shave away from from strolling down a fucking catwalk during Fashion Week. We were finally in an era where it wasn't a rarity to find beautiful women. They were everywhere. Shiiiiiiiiiit, most of them were looking for a sugar daddy, and if you cheated on them, it was just "frowned upon" but nowhere close to a deal breaker. You could get away with murder... *which I also did.*

If someone fucked me on a deal, you could throw the cops a few shekels and they'd look the other way. I had formed some fringe mob ties over the last few years simply because they needed a place to stash their money. What better way to do than the stock market? I had a natural gift for it. Like a cheap diuretic, that shit just came easy to me.

When our country joined World War I, I invested in steel, because everything—planes subs, tanks, and boats—required it. Steel companies were mostly union and controlled by the mob, so investing in it made sense on paper for them, but more importantly, the government. No one thought it was suspicious. It wasn't like Phil Mickelson dropping a mill into a tiny pharma company that magically came up with the cure for Hep C two weeks later or some bullshit. War investments were a long term deal and it worked out well for all of us, and NYC and Jersey were the heart of it all.

After my set was over, I set the piano on fire and proceed to piss out the flames, same as I always do. Fuck, I'm awesome. Another flapper girl asks to smell my fingers when I hopped off stage, and I oblige. I'm not even sure what her end game was on that one or what fetish that might possibly be, but I obviously I let her. Sometimes I deny myself the knowledge in order to give, for when we give—sorry that coke is starting to drip and my mind is in the front seat of a rocket ship right now with no lap belt in sight. I'm riding the fucking rails right now, brother.

"All aboard!" I scream out before dumping out more coke onto my coffee table.

Two beautiful flapper chicks grab my cock as I rip through another scooch of that panty grease. I sit back on the couch as the party rages around me and think to myself, "Does life get any better than this shit right here?" Like most glorious moments in my life, some cocksucker has to roll in and fuck it up. Almost as if it was on cue—

Boom!

The Cops bust the fucking door down and the party screams as if a one-eyed man was on the floor looking for a marble. Son of a bitch. That coke drip is my favorite part of the experience and now it's ruined like a fart in a butterfly jar.

"Saint James Street James, we have to confiscate your alcohol!" One of the cops barks out in a New York accent thicker than chunky Ragu.

"Get fucked by a dumpster, pigshit. You aren't taking my liquor! You can have one of two girls currently grabbing my cock, but you're going to have a gunfight on your hands if you want my hooch," I say as I pull a pistol from my shoulder holster hidden in my sport coat.

"Whoa, whoa, whoa! We don't want things to shake out like this, Street. It's the law now!"

"Come on! What fucking law?"

"Prohibition. It has been fully enacted in the state of New York and it is now illegal to distribute alcohol at parties. It's confined to personal use only."

As I put my gun away and walk over to the bar, I hear something dragging behind me. That's when I realize that one of the flapper chick's hands is still latched on to my dong and she's sliding behind me on the floor. It's her moment and I'm not going to ruin it just because my night got fucked.

I begin to study the bottles on the shelf and the cops look at me in confusion. Glancing up at the top shelf, I grab a bottle of whiskey and stare at it, giving that classic Saint James Street James smirk I've given for the last 186 years. You know it well and I know damn well you're picturing it as I speak.

"Personal use only, huh? Great. I'll start with this one," I say as I unscrew the cap and go full Belushi and down the entire bottle.

I smash it on the floor after I finish and then proceed to down seven other bottles of booze, one by one. The last one I put down was a bottle of gin, which always tastes like shit straight. I never understood anyone who drinks that shit straight or who their fucking audience was with that liquor over the past hundred years, but it was a power move in the moment. You drink an entire bottle of gin; people know you buttfuck on Mondays. I lock eyes with the cop during every last drop letting him feel it too, before smashing the empty bottle against the wall after I was done.

"There. Now there's nothing left to distribute. Go fuck yourself, sincerely Saint James Street James."

"The cocaine is illegal too," he says in a pissed off tone.

"Not if it's prescribed, honch. It's medicinal, I got a scrip for it," I say as I take the prescription from my doctor out of my pocket and throw it in his face.

He angrily picks it up off the ground and reads it aloud, "Do four to eighteen lines every six hours. This will help make your constant erections go down?" The party tries to stifle their laughter.

"It's a serious fucking problem! Walk a mile with my dong before you judge."

They knew the coke was legal, so I walk back over to the couch key bumping the entire way, flapper girl still dong attached. The cops shake their head as I take a hard seat down, never breaking eye contact with them. They knew they couldn't do shit. Cocaine in the early 1900's was like weed in the early 2000's. Even though a law was passed against it, you could still get it prescribed from a "physician" if you knew the right peeps. Obviously with my wealth, I could get anything I wanted... *except for liquor now.*

"Party's over everyone. Don't make me come back here, Saint James," the cop said as he motioned people out with his night stick.

As the party begins to exit, I exhale deeply and look skyward trying to ignore the replica Sistine Chapel I had painted on the ceiling. It was time to look inward and really absorb what I was going to do about not having booze. This is the second worst day in my life, besides my family of eight burning to death in that house fire obviously, which was now more than fifty years ago. Actually, I'm sorry, there was a worse day than that, which I'll get to later.

Speaking of which, quick side note on the replica Sistine Chapel thing, I did have the artist switch out all of the religious figures with the Asian prostitutes who died in my poppy fields, and also my kids and shit. I demanded that the nude figures touching index fingers were me and Louretta. My sweet Loubo. He really captured her thick, full, red bush exquisitely—and that meant the world to me. The whole thing looks pretty rad. Also, it's nice to have your whole original family looking down on you as you bone complete stranger's night after night having little to no conscience.

"You okay boss?" A familiar voice calls out from one of my 19 bathrooms.

I look over and see Samantha Davis, my Chinaman, buckling up his belt as he shuffles out into the living room. He's now 111 years old, and looks every goddamn last second of it. At the time, he was the oldest living man in America. Al Roker would have re-sharted himself to have this fucker's pic on a bottle of Smucker's on the *Today Show* if it had existed back then. His face has more divots than a rock climbing wall inside an REI. It's amazing he's still alive, frankly. His work ethic is still there, and he's made a pretty decent butler for me since we arrived in New York—however I avoid watching him walk up all those steps to change my bed sheets every day, simply because it bores me. As he walks over to me, I hold up my hand motioning him to stop.

"Hey bro, your dork and balls are hanging out of your pants. You want to tuck those in and zip that up, chief?"

"Sorry boss, let me grab my stick," he says with a half smile.

He pulls out an old wooden "knitter's pride" shawl stick from his back pocket and begins to weave it through his elongated ball sack four times before placing it back inside his pants. Homeboy is 111 years old, those balls are holding on for dear life in that sack like a fat girl on a rope swing down by a river. His lack of not being rich at an early enough age has caused him to age horrifically. Being poor really takes a toll on your scroat. He finally finishes and sits down next to me, propping his feet up on the girl laying on the floor with an arm still attached to my hog.

"What happened to the party boss? You run out of booze?"

"Sort of. The fucking cops busted in and and starting screaming about Prohibition and—you didn't hear any of that shit?"

He shakes his head. "What happened to the party boss? You run out of booze?"

Christ. He can't hear shit anymore. It honestly makes me sad. After all these years we've spent together, it looks like it's finally time to get a new butler. I'm sure he'll find work elsewhere. As he stares straight ahead with that constant old man Chinese half smile that they all give, I decide to slide this chick's hand over to his dong. God knows he could use it more than me right now.

I get up and walk over to the window looking out over the city. My lady New York. Down below I see a gimpy shop owner getting the shit kicked out of him by a handful of mobsters. The dude looks like a "Ron". I hear him muster out the usual, "Please stop, I have a wife and kids," line before he falls to his knees on the sidewalk. They pry a wooden crate out of his quivering hands as blood pours from his face. One of the mob guys pulls out a crow bar and knocks him unconscious with a final blow to the dome before applying it to the crate. Nighty night *Ron*.

A couple quick pops and that fucker rips open revealing about twelve bottles of booze. It was brown, and I was fucking down. They smile at one another before loading the crate into the back of a Model T. I open up the window and yell down to them.

"How much for that Easus Jesus?"

They all look up at me annoyed. "The what?" One of them yells back.

"That wine vagine. I'm looking to buy that case of Kentucky cough syrup you just stuffed into the back of your ride there, holmes."

"This is for someone else," the mobster yells back.

"Is that someone else about nine inches tall?" I ask as I slam the window shut and quickly drop my pants and slap my dong against the glass. "This someone will be right down."

I zip up my shit and walk over to take the elevator downstairs. I look at Sam whose face is still frozen at "Asian half-smile" staring straight ahead at the wall. The flapper girl is still attached to his cock. Is she sleeping? Waiting for me to come back? Does she have a rare degenerative disease that causes her hand to clamp down on units? So many fucking questions at this point, but I'll need at least one more drink for an answer.

I walk out the front door to the four pissed off mobsters standing there looking like they want to beat my ass. One of them taps the crow bar in his hands, two of them hold Tommy guns, and the other holds up half an axe handle. Why not just bring the whole axe? Super weird flex at that moment.

"What are you, some kind of doo-doo chaser? A fucking queer?" He asks.

"I knew my meat stick would get your attention—

"Why don't you show him what we do to faguettes in this neighborhood, Johnny?"

He points to Johnny, the large Italian man in his 40's, holding the half axe handle. Johnny taps it in the palm of his hand and smiles as he walks over to me. In a rather labored motion, he swings it down at me with brute force. I calmly step aside, and then throat chop him, sending him to his knees. The smaller, stout, Italian man with the crow bar runs at me quickly and tries to take a swipe at my knees. I jump over it faster than a black girl in Harlem mid Double-Dutch, and knock this motherfucker out.

The two men holding Tommy guns, smile. "That was a nice show. We each enjoyed it, but where was the tap dance portion?" He asks as he opens fire at the concrete next to my feet.

Saint James Street James dances for no man. Matter of fact, I don't even move one single inch. As his round empties, he stares at me in shock. The other Italian gangster tries to squeeze the trigger on his smoke hammer, but I've already pulled out my pearl handled six shooter and put a bullet in his brain. Even though we have relatively decent firearms now, I still never strayed from my pistols in the 1800's.

The mobster who talked all that shit and is now out of pussy ammo for his Tommy gun, and he retreats toward his car as fast as he can. I grab him by the neck and pistol whip him to the ground. Blood streams out of his forehead as he stares up at me from the concrete in fear. A few lights from the neighbors flick on and people hover by their windows concerned. Shit didn't go down like this too often in a rich ass neighborhood like mine.

"You better not kill me! I know people!" he screams.

With a little better lighting now on my face, I step over him so he can see my whole shit.

"Turn the fucking lights off neighbors or all your wives get fucked!" Everyone obliges at the same exact time as I smile back down to the man on the ground. "Looks like I know people too."

I reach into my pocket and pull out a thousand in cash and slap it down on his chest, then casually walk over to the back of his car and grab the case of whiskey. You already know daddy takes a bottle out and samples the merch. Damn. That's some good Congressman's coffee. I holster my six shooter and walk toward the front of my house.

"Tell all the 'people that you know' that you met me tonight and that there's plenty more lettuce to go with that whiskey. It never hurts to have more green in your diet. And take the dead guy with you. Trash isn't being picked up until next Monday and I don't want an Italian on concrete wafting through the street. That's a sandwich reference I just made, because you guys fucking stink."

As the door shuts behind me, I can see him get up and scoop up his dead friend as quickly as possible. The other two come to life and stumble into the car as homeboy cranks the engine. He leans out of the driver side window and screams.

"We'll see yous real fucking soon!"

That was the point. Also, way to fit the stereotype. I smile as I look down at the whiskey inside the crate when the elevator door opens. It's funny, right before the 1920's the mob started gaining more and more control of the city. Local businesses, bars, whore joints—any operation that could turn a quick buck that was owned by weak people, they had control of so they could take their cut. Now me, I was a stock market guy, I didn't give shit so I always turned a blind eye to it. Kill people if they fuck with you has always been, and will always, be my motto. If you're weak enough to let that shit happen to you, well then you fucking deserve that walk with the reaper.

I know what you're thinking, "But Saint James Street James, weren't you worried about the cops coming back?" Fuck no. Truth is, the cops cared more about drinking booze than mob killings back in the day, so I knew I could wax that greasy wop on the street and get away with it. Hell, I was actually *doing them a favor*. I also knew they would roll that fat prick into their boss's office and he'd be forced to deal with me directly. I need that liquor, son. My doctor could prescribe coke to me on the reg, but booze was a no go? Fuck that noise.

I place the crate full of whiskey on the ground and take the open bottle I was sipping on downstairs and head toward the couch. The flapper girl was still latched onto Sam's dick. I hand him the open bottle and his half smile turns full. He takes a swill and looks up at me.

"You kill someone?" He asks.

"You know that answer, Sam. Someone will be by in the morning looking for me I'm sure. Obviously, make them wait until nooner. I forgot that I drank those seven bottles earlier, so I'm going to need a few extra winks tonight."

"Sure thing boss."

"You there on the floor, what's your fucking deal?" I say to the flapper girl on the ground.

Without looking up she says, "My father was a rock climber. He died while I was attached to him. I still have a hard time letting go."

"Fair enough. Sam you cool with it?"

"It helps me sleep boss," he says with a smile as he leans his head back and takes a sip of whiskey.

"I'll allow it. Goodnight to you both."

As I walk over to the stairs, I stop by yet another nude painting of Louretta, rub two fingers across her bush, and take a deep inhale. Goddamnit I miss it. I went through 36 different artists to make it a scratch and sniff. Pablo Picasso finally got the smell right. The Spaniards sure know the scent of a woman's beaver.

Chapter 2

DON'T MAKE ME TELL
YOU TWICE

I hear the shades slowly being pulled open in my room followed by the sweet sound of awe from an Asian. We all know that sound. Fucking Samantha Davis is here to lift my black out shades to gently wake me, which means there's someone at the front door. I rub my eyes and slowly lift the sheets to stand up, but I can't. This fucking girl has her hand on my dick again somehow. What is with this chick? This is just pure insanity at this point. Luckily, there's a nude gold statue of myself that I had made to match my son's—including my full dong—directly next to my bed, so I place her hand on that.

I squint as I move to the side of the bed and look up at Sam. "What time is it?"

"It's 3pm. There are some mob guys here waiting at the front door," he says as he shuffles to the next seven windows in my master bedroom to pull open the shades.

"How long have they been here?"

"Since 8am. They don't look happy, boss."

"Okay. Tell them to wait two more hours while I take a cock soak. You know I can't function after a bender without one."

He smiles. "I know. You want me to have this weird girl join you? I can walk her in while you relax?"

"No, that won't be necessary. The daddy issues thing is cool, but I wish her father died raising a flag instead of stuck to a rock, you know what I'm saying?" I ask as I make a jack off motion with my hand in case he's too old to get it.

"I understand. I'll leave her attached to your golden dick. You want me to come with you today?"

"Yeah, you sure you're feeling up to it?"

"At this age, I feel like dying every day, so it really doesn't matter where I am."

"Great. Can you walk down all 167 stairs and grab me a glass of whiskey while I bathe my body?"

"Of course. I wouldn't dream of relaxing at my advanced age."

"Perfect. Try not to shake so much and spill it on the way up," I say as I disrobe and walk into the bathroom.

As water pours out of the mouth of my customized 24 carat gold Egyptian Sphinx faucet, I ponder the meeting that will take place as I stretch out in the tub. People know who the fuck I am financially in this town, but my Wild West days of recognition are far behind me, which sucks in situations like this. The fear and intimidation factor walking into a room where everyone knows I could kill them with a flick of my steel comes in real fucking handy. Most importantly, it made people more reluctant to do dumb shit.

Sure I'm rich as fuck, but let's face it; no one is scared of your wallet. Take your average lawyer today—someone you went to high school with for example—why did he become a lawyer? Simple. He's a fucking pussy who wanted to have a little bit of bread in his pocket and use lawsuits to hide behind his lack of masculinity. A guy like me could dog walk these motherfuckers in front of their wife and kids in a highly populated public area and there's nothing they could do about it... *except sue two weeks later.*

Imagine having to look your wife and kids in the eye forever after some shit like that and pretend "you're in charge" at your own house. Not a goddamn prayer. Your daughter will grow up to blow a dude in front of you just because she can. That's why a huge wallet doesn't really mean shit in the grand scheme of things if you're not a goddamn man.

At least the mob has honor, but it comes at a price. I can't just buy my way in, something fucked up is going to go down for me to prove my loyalty and that I'm not a fucking snitch. I just don't know what that's going to be. I'll obviously strap up with my two pearl handled pistols holstered up high and tight, but those will be taken the second I walk in. The thing about these Italians is they love to talk, so there's no doubt homeboy from last night regaled them of my quick draw skills. My guns will be the first things they take. I thought about taking a knife, but that's some homeless "tent village" shit, so I scrap that plan.

As I step out of the tub two hours later, Samantha wraps me in a towel made of real Egyptian hair. Whose hair is it? Don't give a shit. It just feels rich and that's what's important. Time to get suited and booted. As I put on my five-thousand-dollar suit with gold cufflinks, I look at myself in the mirror as Sam dusts off my shoulders.

"At least I'll look better than these fucking guidos," I say to him.

"Indeed sir. You sure are a dapper man."

"You got a bump for me brother?"

He shakes his head and reaches into his pocket. "Of course. It's almost 5pm. So sorry, I don't know what I was thinking."

He pulls out a tiny gold spoon and reaches into a bag for a generous key bump for me to devour. I take a strong toot, then point to my other nostril. It catches him off guard.

"This shotgun is a double barrel my dude."

"Oooooohhhhh, you going real hard today."

"You never know how shit is going to shake out. One thing is for certain, I'd hate to die with a full bag of coke on me. That would be like dying mid-way through a blow job. You want some nose candy, Sam?"

"Of course," he says with a smile.

I watch him as he blasts two pile drivers into his head holes and stumble backward. Before I laugh in his face, I grab his arm to keep him from falling. Damn. Father time is a real bitch to some people. I used to blast the white squall with this motherfucker for hours, now he's reduced to being the oldest guy in the movie *Cocoon*. I take the bag from him and tuck it back in my pocket. One more toot for him could be catastrophic.

As we walk out of the bathroom and hit the first step on the staircase, his knees buckle. This yayo ain't for dudes this old, especially after the drip kicks in. He tries to steady himself along the handrail, but barely makes it down one full step. This shit is sad to see. At this rate, we wouldn't make the meeting until the middle of next week. I decide to pick him up and carry him down, because I knew he'd be too proud to ask. As I lift him, he objects—

"Boss, please. It is I who should be carrying you. I actually did carry you up the stairs all these years."

"It's time for me to repay the favor. When I open the door, you have to stand on your own though. I need these fucks to be curious of why I roll with a wise old Chinaman."

"You think I'm wise?"

"No. You're dumb as shit, but you're my only friend left. Just continue to squint and nod slowly when we get to wherever we're going. It fools every white person."

"That part comes naturally," he says as he points at his slanted eyes.

We share a laugh as I continue to carry him down the the stairs. He smiles as wide as the Great Wall of China. Sorry, that's probably a little too on the nose. What-the-fuck-ever, it's a nice moment. He's so goddamn frail at this stage of his life, I'm not sure how many moments we'll have left like this together. When we hit the front door, I set him down and he nods that he's ready to go as he regains his sea legs.

I pull open the doors to my house and see the one mouthy Italian dude from last night and another fat Italian in his 40's sitting on my front stoop. The fat Italian stands up and turns around, and I see that he's missing his nose partially. It almost looks like a pig nose. Matter of fact, there's hardly any skin around his nostrils at all. I recoil in disgust.

"Don't even think about asking me for coke, piggy," I say.

"That's hilarious. We'll see how funny you are when you meet the boss," he says in a thick Italian accent.

"Get in the car," the other one says as he points to the vehicle he peeled off in last night after I killed his friend.

"No, my driver will take me," I say as I point to Sam.

The little one leans into me. "You sure? It'd be a shame to lose your life and your ride in the same day," he says with a condescending chuckle.

"Believe me, I'm planning on losing the ride. My life will remain to be seen. We'll follow you. Sam, you ready?"

These fucking lower level Italian guys exchange confused glances as I hand my keys to Samantha. They cautiously walk to their car as Sam and I walk across the street to mine. Sam opens up the passenger door for me and I slide in like a smooth goose. He then walks around and jumps in the driver's seat, looking up at me nervously before starting the engine.

"You sure you want me to drive boss? You haven't let me drive in over forty years."

"That's because you're old *and* Asian. That's a deadly combo in an era like this, or any other era for that matter. Remember how you used to fuck up those wagons back in the day?"

"I do love to drive," he says with a laugh as he longingly touches the steering wheel.

"Then do your worst. Follow these pricks."

Sam fires up the ignition as I lay on the horn and start screaming at the Italians, "Let's go you greasy fucks! I don't have all day!"

They start up their car and pull out as Sam pulls out right behind them. So far so good for about ten feet, until he veers off the side of the road and begins to hit every parked car against the curb he passes. The Italian guys look back in horror as I smile and put my hand underneath the wheel, unbeknownst to Sam, to give him a little guidance. Not much. Just enough so we don't get killed. After 40 years without steering some form of wagon or car, I do let him nuke a good deal of a hundred or so cars all the way to the mob boss' place. Yolo.

The car dies and smoke pours from the engine as we stop in front of a warehouse downtown. My car is now completely smashed to shit. The fucking thing is absolutely totaled. Sam beams from sea to shining sea. The mob guys get out and look at us in shock as I act as if nothing has happened.

"You let this slant total your Model T?"

"I told you I wasn't planning on leaving with it. Here," I say as I flip him the keys. He stops not really knowing what to do next. I clap my hands in front of his face. "Well, are you going to take me inside the ominous warehouse or am I going to stand outside with my dick in my hand?"

The Italians knock twice on the door and metal door over a peep hole pushes to the right, where we see a set of eyes nod with acknowledgement. Another fucking peephole. My life is filled with them. Probably because I've always been doing corrupt and immoral shit. The only people who need peep holes in this life are criminals. When the door opens, I'm greeted by what seems to be every single Jersey Mike's manager I've ever met in my entire life. Two fat fucks in cheap suits begin frisking me and Sam.

"I'll spare you the shock, I'm packing two pistols," I say with my hands slightly raised.

The fat Italian man who already grazed my dick pulls out both of my pearl handled six shooters and stares at them with amazement. He looks at me puzzled. "Were you in the Wild fucking West or something?"

This remark elicits laughter that echoes through the large warehouse. What am I supposed to say, that I'm 96 years old right now but I've been rich enough to beat the natural human aging process? No one will believe me, so instead, I make up a quick story.

"My grandfather gave them to me. He said the only thing a man should ever need to carry in this life is a pistol.

You carry anything else and your compensating for having a small dick."

A few of the men with Tommy guns cough loudly and politely hide their weapons behind their back. Suddenly, a light from the back of the warehouse turns on illuminating the entire place where. I see a man in his 50's, Joe the Boss, approach. He's different from the rest of these assholes in the fact that he looks and sounds like he is actually still in Italy.

"You the guy who killed my man?" He asks.

"I'm not the guy who fucked him, that's for damn sure."

Everyone's eyes grow wide as Joe takes this in. "That's cute. He was one of my best men."

"He couldn't have been that goddamn great or he'd still be alive right now."

Joe picks up his pace as he slowly approaches me. "Tell me why I shouldn't kill you right now?"

"Because *you* can't. I see a lot of guys with bullshit toy guns who theoretically could, but what's the fun in killing an unarmed man?"

"There's a lot a fun in killing—

I step in closer to him now and go nose to nose. "Not if you can't do it yourself. You can send someone to kill for you, but you're not the one pulling the trigger seeing the brain matter splattered against the wall. When you can see the entire cerebrum shat out into the side of a kitchen cabinet or the Broca area dripping from the ceiling of a whorehouse, then it's fun. Fifteen guys in a firing squad with semi-automatics is fucking boring, and frankly, a little bitch like."

"What's your end game here?"

"I want in. Booze. You got it, and I fucking need it. I got half the city investing with me, but I need to keep throwing parties for other rich folk like myself. They have a good time, they invest. Simple as that. You can't have a good time without booze and coke my man."

"That's the fucking truth," he says as everyone nods in agreement. "So why did you kill my man? If you wanted to buy alcohol, I would have had no problem selling it to a rich fuck like you."

"You had four guys out in the street last night for one single crate of giggle water. That tells me you aren't making enough of it, or don't have access to it. You need a cash infusion to keep that whiskey flowing. More men. Since alcohol is now considered a crime, you have to be more organized. This shit can be extremely lucrative if we're the only game in town."

"We? Let's get something straight. There is no *we*," he says.

"There's too much money to lose if there is no *we*. This small time shit with fifteen dudes ain't going to cut it. You have to scale. Otherwise you're going to go dry real fucking quick. All of us are."

He mulls it over as he looks around at his crew. I can tell he knows that I'm right. "We don't let bankers into the Little Five Points gang."

"The Little Five Points Gang? Christ. We should definitely change the name of that. It sounds like five dudes docking boners in an astrology pattern. What's the criteria for joining your little gang?"

"Offing someone," he says rather stone cold.

"That's it? Shit, every morning I wake up I got murder on my mind."

"Great. Then you'll have no problem killing this guy right here."

He snaps his fingers and two more fat Italians bring out some kid who looks like he's been crying into a tit or caught stealing condoms from a candy shop owner. There's no way he's a day over twenty. A large wood chipper suddenly roars to life inside the warehouse. Almost as if it was on some sort of mafia cue, a spotlight flickers to life above it.

"Did you buy this whole warehouse just to store one wood chipper? Because there is literally nothing else in here but this *one wood chipper.*"

"Shut the fuck up. You want in or not? Show me what your made of."

I take off my coat and drop it on the floor, then casually start rolling up my sleeves. I walk over to the kid, who clearly looks like he's about to shit his pants. He pleads at me with his eyes underneath his newsboy hat. I lightly slap his face.

"I'm not killing him—

"I fucking knew it!" Joe screams.

"He's what, eighteen? Nineteen tops? How old are you kid?"

"I'm almost twenty, sir."

"Do you know me?"

"No," he says meekly.

"I don't know you either," I say as I turn toward Joe. "Which is why this shouldn't be part of your initiation. Anyone can kill a stranger. Someone they don't know. What you want is a guy who can kill someone they actually know. Someone close to to them. Then it really means something. It means they will do anything for you."

I turn toward Samantha and our eyes lock. He's so old he can barely stand up for this amount of time. It fucking sucks to see him like this. Sam gives a slight nod to me and I walk over to him. I grab him by the shoulders and look into his eyes intently.

"Now this man. I've been friends with him for fifty fucking years. He's been my right hand man in all of my endeavors."

"Jesus Christ how old are you?"

"Shut the fuck up! This man who I've known forever, who has been my closest *compadre*, is the man you should be asking me to kill. Not some dime store hoodlum who swiped a couple caramels to give to his grandma to stop her from sucking dick for money."

I never break eye contact with Sam. Memories of the first time we struck gold together in 1849, traveling to China to bring back opium and whores for six years, to finishing the Transcontinental Railroad together— come flooding back to me. I grit my teeth and move in closer.

Just below a ventriloquist whisper I push out the words, "Do you want me to end it?"

He nods, wanting his time on earth to come t a close. "Twice," he whispers back.

Son of a bitch. He wants to die just like his father. I'll never forget that story he told me when we were working on his boat before we sailed overseas. Mostly because that story is super fucked up and I've never met anyone who saw someone get killed by the same swordfish leaping through the air to spear a man to death in the heart two times. That goddamn thing really did want to kill him. It was time to honor my best friend the same way.

I pick him up over my head as the Italians look on in utter disbelief. As I carry him over to the wood chipper, he lets out a long exhale as if he's relieved. Truthfully, I wouldn't want to keep living either if I was in this type of condition, or if my boner stopped working. I know this is what he wants, to die with dignity, so I hoist him into the air. He screams out to the Italians with all his might—

"You rike it?!!"

I was surprised how quickly his body went through the blades and shot out the other side. Jesus. I was definitely not expecting it to go *that* fast. Part of me thought it would be like a giant log kind of sputtering around before it caught the right angle—I don't know man. I spot a large industrial broom against the wall behind the wood chipper and begin sweeping up his chopped up body parts. Joe the Boss stops me.

"Hey man, we're good. It's not necessary to clean this up. You've proved yourself to me."

"But I'm not done. You see, it's important to double check everything these days, you understand? Everyone must be checked out *twice*."

I continue to sweep his body parts back together, then pick up the pieces with my bare hands, walking with his guts around to the front of the wood chipper, which is still going. It's a goddamn mess. I then heave his parts back into the wood chipper and they shoot out even faster this time. The floor looks like a Jackson Pollock painting. A few of the Italians begin vomiting all over the floor. I'm covered in Sam's blood, staring directly at Joe. After a few seconds, he nods his head impressed. He smiles and lights a cigar.

"So how much money can you invest?"

"How about we start with one million?"

"Get the fuck out of here. You got a million in your bank?"

"I got fifteen. One million will be to start. Make sure you don't fuck up anything and I'll put in more. I'll have it by Friday. Have this kid come pick it up," I say pointing to the boy he asked me to kill.

He laughs. "Yeah, fuck it, I'll have him drive you home if you want? Your driver ain't going to be able to now."

Everybody roars with laughter. I fake a smile, but deep down, it's hard. I just lost my best friend. Shit, he was the only friend I've had for that long in my entire life. As Joe and the rest of the Italians start to exit the warehouse, I look over to the kid. He looks like he just saw his grandmother masturbating in the shower, he's that shook up. I pick up my suit coat off the warehouse floor and walk over to the broom and sweep up the rest of Samantha Davis' remains. The kid tries to stop me—

"You don't have to do that, someone else will do that," he says.

"No. It's my mess, I'll clean it up."

I lay down my coat and spread it open, sweeping his chopped up body inside of it. When I finish, I tie off the remains with the arms of the coat and tuck them under my left arm. He walks over and attempts to shake my hand, but is unsure how to proceed with so much blood covering it.

"I just—I just want to thank you for saving my life. I'm eternally grateful," he says nervously.

"You don't have to shake my fucking hand. It shows weakness. Plus, I'm covered in a hundred-year-old man's *probable* lower intestines. A ride will suffice," I say as I begin to walk out.

"I can take you where ever you want to go. Where are you headed?"

"Chinatown."

"Of course. Forgive me," he says as he nervously points to my balled up jacket under my arm.

"That's racist."

"I'm sorry, that was bad," he backtracks.

"Stop apologizing. I don't give a fuck. I'm going there for something else that's none of your goddamn business. What's your name?"

"Alphonse. Alphonse Capone."

"Definitely shorten that first name, chief. You sound like a black clarinet player at the Cotton Club. Now take me to Chinatown, Al."

Chapter 3
FRY SO HIGH

I roll down the windows of Capone's car as we head into Chinatown, so I could let that sweet scent of squirrel di slap me right in the face. I was happier than Morgan Freeman rolling down that fucking bus window in *Shawshank Redemption* on the way to Zihuatanejo. Prosties danced in windows, old Chinamen cut the heads off of ducks, 8 year-olds were chain smoking—everything reminded me of him. That's why tonight is going to be *his* night. My sweet Samantha Davis is going home, I thought to myself as I tap his shredded up body stuffed inside my sport coat.

"Here is fine," I say to Al, motioning for him to pull over.

"You sure?" He asks as he sees a dog get stabbed in the middle of the street and drug over to a barrel fire to be cooked.

"Yeah, I'm good. These are my people. You got a heater I can have to go? I left mine in my jacket and they're a bit wet."

"Sure," he says as he reaches into his jacket and pulls out a coffin nail for me.

"See you Friday, fuckface," I say as I light it up and blow a huge cloud of smoke into his face upon exiting the vehicle.

I walk over to a street meat vendor and ask for a stick of squirrel di. As I eat this delicious meat, I wander through the streets doing bumps of cocaine here and there, taking hits off random opium pipes with an old Chinaman washing himself in a trough, and drinking sake in back alleys. It feels like my backyard in Coloma again.

After a few hours of working up a goddamn near black out level buzz, I take the rolled up Samantha in my sport coat into a whorehouse. The sounds of pan flutes and wind chimes begin wafting out of the windows. I have enough cash on me to get weird, so why the fuck not? The loss of my best friend took a toll on me mentally that I wasn't really prepared for.

Look, old people die—except me—and I understand that. It really was his time to go. One can argue that maybe a wood chipper *isn't* the best way to go, but from a business stand point it gave me power. Anyone willing to *Fargo* their best friend twice is not a man to be fucked with, but it still didn't make it any easier. Since tonight is about him, I decide to let Samantha Davis watch one last time. He would have wanted this.

When I walk through the doors, an older Chinese broad with a gong, bangs it loudly and claps her hands two times, forcefully. It's not like the "Nicole Kidman clapping at an award show" type of way. No, she wants these ladies to stop doing their nails and come out to meet their potential suitor. Prostitution was huge in NYC back in the day... *and it was glorious.*

As a matter of fact, that shit really didn't stop here until the late 90's. I could get a decent jerk sesh from a prosty in a back alley for forty right up until about 98', until that asshole Giuliani took over. Congrats on the one thousandth Starbucks opening where every bathroom is now genderless. I could rage on this for days, but if you need a "fuck boi culture marker" in NYC, it was right after WUTANG decided to do movies and shit. McSorley's is the only *real* place left after Elaine's shut down on 81st. No lie.

As China's finest quickly shuffled out to greet me, I saw the nervous excitement on their faces when I swung it against my leg. Much the same way they eagerly anticipated my pork dagger back in China when Samantha and I traveled over there together and I left him and my entire family for six years. Tonight really isn't about me though, and I decide to do what I thought he would have wanted me to do—which was to fuck them all.

"I'll take the whole lot," I drunkenly blurt out to the madam.

"But sir, I would have to shut down for the night. That would take a king's ransom," she says.

"Luckily, my head is fucking heavy, because I am wearing the crown," I say as I pull out a wad of cash from of my pocket that would make 2 Chainz blush.

I throw it high into the air and it starts pouring down on them like the first wave to hit the boat in *The Perfect Storm*. The madam gives me a *Benihana's* waitress smile like I held up a credit card and said "same bill" at the end of a meal. She expertly moves in behind me and locks the front door before flipping the window sign over to read "Closed."

"What's your name?" I ask her.

"Yuki," she replies. "I will take care of you tonight. Any special requests?"

My eyes well up as I point to my rolled up sport coat underneath my arm. "Yes, I want him to watch me screw one last time. He was one of you."

She smiles and nods. "I understand."

At the time, I obviously thought I was in some small sort of rational state. Looking back at it now, I know how completely fucked up it was asking a stranger to make sure my buddy—who I murdered by throwing him into a wood chipper *twice*—might find it off putting. Like I've said in the last two books, Asians have a better culture than us. They respect the dead and other people's wishes and shit better than Americans, which I dig.

Yuki took my rolled up sport coat and places it on a rolling cart, before slowly taking off my clothes. Now completely nude, she smiles and gives a head nod to the other girls to lead me to the back. I could hear the wheels of the rolling cart carrying Samantha's dead body spinning right behind me. It felt like I was back in China again… *my second home.*

The first room I was taken to had a koi pond inside of it. I have never seen anything like it in America during the 1920's, and I have seen some rich ass shit. The Asian women sit me down on a set of down pillows in front of the pond and begin massaging my shoulders as I stare into the water. Yuki pulls the cart up next to me and kneels down.

"Your friend, he died an honorable death or else you would not have brought him here, yes?"

"Yes, Yuki. He enjoyed the most out of this life that he could, based on height, weight, race, and gender during this time period."

"Goo. That's real goo. Let's take you back to your happiest memories with him and send him home properly tonight," Yuki whispers before shoving a lime in my ass.

I wince, as it was obviously uncomfortable. Strange way to start off an orgy I thought, but then it dawns on me. Sam had jammed a lime up my ass on the boat back when I had scurvy en route to China. I let it ease in without a fight, before turning to her—

"How did you know?"

"Shhhhhh. You knocked up my grandmother who was working for you in your opium fields back in California a long time ago. You know my father, Yolo."

Holy shit. Every single Asian person really does know each other. Also, I said his name earlier in the book in complete irony now. Fuck me. Before I'm able to speak, she points to a grainy picture on the wall of me from the 1850's.

Son of a bitch. I'm even a goddamn legend now close to 70 years later. She smiles so big her eyes *almost* turn round.

"How is Yolo? That was a weird night to be honest. I don't think I saw him since he was riding on that horse covered in blood through that makeshift orgy moments after he was born," I say.

"Yolo only lived once. He found that out the hard way when he tried to make the first hand glider out of paper," she says with sadness in her voice. "We didn't know rain was in the forecast that day."

"That happens. So… am I getting fucked or am I fucking other people?" I ask quickly trying to change the subject because it's a fucking downer.

"Both, but tonight is about rediscovery of one's self."

"What does that mean? Because I'm not tucking my own dick into my ass if that's what you're saying?"

"No," she giggles. "It's time to take him back home… and take *you* back home too. It's been far too long."

As she finishes the massage, she hands me an opium pipe to take a hit off of. She then places the sport coat with Sam in it under my arm as she moves around the back of the table where my feet are. Slowly, she begins to raise the entire table above her head. The immense amount of oil that is covering every square inch of my body causes my momentum to move forward into the koi pond. I grip the remains of Samantha and look back at her in panic.

"What the fuck is going on?"

"Swim under to the other side. Your journey awaits. Hold on to him," she says as she points to Samantha.

Before I can say another word, I'm submerged in water. I open my eyes and see koi fish quickly retreat. The blood from Samantha's remains has now quickly mixed in and turned the water into a pinkish red. In front of me I can see a white light, so I swim towards it. For some reason the panic within me was gone, maybe because at this point I thought I was dead. Little did I know, I was actually about to be free.

I doggy paddle through the murky water, and the light becomes brighter to the point where I see what appears to be grass reeds growing upward. Like a horror film, I grab a handful and begin to pull myself up, gasping loudly for air before finally hit the top of a surface. I'm not going to overact like a housewife at a half off sale at *Hobby Lobby*, but it felt like a long goddamn time. On hardcore drugs, everything feels like an eternity though.

Peeking through the reeds, I can see ten beautiful Asian women working diligently in rice paddies. Holy fuck. It's exactly like the first time Sam's boat pulled into China all those years ago. A couple of the ladies spot me and pull my body through the reeds. As they tug my right arm, I see more blood stream from the sport coat in the shallow water. The women eventually rest my body on a large mound of dirt. I'm nude, oiled up, covered in mud, and gripping a shredded dead body. Am I in another world? Did they *really* dig a hole to China? Is it possible they laced some DMT in the opium?

Is the woman taking a shit in front of me a power move or something to be disgusted by?

I blink my eyes and snap out of it. The woman that appeared to be taking a shit in front of me was simply squatting down to take off some sort of waders. Within seconds, the other women followed suit. One of the women pulls on a large rope dangling from the ceiling, that set off a trap door like effect, exposing the sky. I can now see the moon, who shrugs at me. Even this motherfucker didn't have an answer.

As the moonlight brightens my surroundings, I realize I was inside a large warehouse that is built like the rice paddy fields over in China. *Epcot Center* can go fuck itself, this is the most realistic shit I've ever seen. This was some first rate whoremanship.

I marvel at my surroundings as two Chinese pond herons walk by and sit next to me staring out over the water. Yup. You read that right. They fucking brought wildlife over here to enhance the ambiance. I WAS IN CHINA. The vividly detailed lengths they went to were amazing.

Women slowly begin walking up in groups of twos. One would straddle me, while the other would bring forward a Chinese flower to Samantha. I recognize the first flowers laid under what appears to be what is left of Samantha's feet. They were plum blossoms, considered to be a "friend of winter", which are symbols of endurance. Let's face it, there isn't a motherfucker on this earth who endured more fucked up shit than Samantha. The reason I knew so much about these flowers was because she told me out loud.

"THESE ARE PLUM BLOSSOMS, CONSIDERED TO BE A FRIEND OF WINTER, WHICH ARE SYMBOLS OF ENDURANCE," she screams.

Otherwise, I never would have known. As soon as these words escape her lips, I had some of the most intense sex I've ever had in my life as one by one they came over to pay their respects, not only to Sam, but also my grieving dong. Piles of flowers were laid out onto the makeshift raft underneath his body parts until they eventually covered him. Loud drumming begins to play from within the grass reeds, heightening the sex. There's nothing like being scored to live music while you're fucking. It really does add a cinematic feel to it, which I highly recommend if you're extremely rich.

As the drumming grows louder, I was startled when I look out across the warehouse and see forty or so bald, Chinese men in their 50's playing those little tiny *Karate Kid II* drums in unison. Look, I'm use to hairless Asian men, but these motherfuckers went "Full Fulcrum.[3]" Beads of water run down their bodies effortlessly. Did I have questions? *Sure.* But this wasn't the time. Instead, I put my head back down and enjoy the magic.

As the last twosome walk up, the first girl gently squats down on me. I notice the last remaining girl is holding a Chinese lantern. It was the exact same lantern that Samantha had made for my dead wife and kids who burned up in that

---

3 Full Fulcrum is named after Nathaniel Francis Fulcrum, a gay ballet dancer from Poland who believed that having sex with a fully shaved man was virtually the same as having sex with a woman. He is entirely incorrect in his theory and often used this excuse just to fuck more dudes.

house fire years ago and cast it out into my river. She ties the lantern down to the makeshift bamboo raft and sparks some type of flint creating a flame. The raft with Sam's body started drifting slowly toward the open doors of the roof before eventually making its way into the open sky.

I look at the moon who nods, telling me it was time to climax, so I grabbed two handfuls of soil beneath me and oblige. The moon and I have always shared a special kinship, and more importantly, I trusted him. I let out a Viking scream as I yeet, never breaking eye contact with the moon. The reverb off the walls shakes the bottom of the raft and some of the Chinese flowers rain down on me. Again, I really can't emphasize what the musical score meant in this moment, but goddamnit this atmosphere is electric. It was like a cross between *Coraline* and *Apocalypse Now* up in this piece. The night was truly awe inspiring... for everyone except Samantha *obviously.*

I follow his remains with my eyes until I can no longer see them. The gravity of the day sinks in and I throw my arms above my head. The women all gather together and politely pull me out of the soil down a hallway into a hot shower. As I stand there, soil washing down my legs between my toes, they begin flogging me with more flowers. When the flogging sesh was over, the drain looked like a freshly planted cedar keyhole garden.

They then quickly dry me off and place me into a karate gei, before walking me down another hallway where I smell that unmistakable scent... *hibachi*. Goddamnit I love these people. When they open the doors, a nude Chinese female chef smiles and points at one solemn chair in front of her, the perfect table for one. It was exactly like my first night in China all those years ago. I inhale deeply and feel a strange sense of calm wash over me. For the first time in my life, I take the time to enjoy the lighting of the onion volcano, instead of violently pulling my head back like JFK in that convertible. Tonight, I appreciate the craft that goes into the art of lighting oil on fire.

Eighteen bottles of sake later, and what seems like four large portions of what today is commonly known as *Rocky's Special*[4], I tear off the belt of my karate gei and stand up from the table stumbling backward into a waiting rickshaw. One of the freshly shaven man drummers takes off full speed as soon as my ass hits the wooden slats out of the back of the room, crashing through two giant doors out into the alley. I steady myself as I clutch a white porcelain bottle of sake, somehow managing to sit upward in my seat.

As this stout Chinaman in his 50's pulls me through the city, I look up and see Samantha's body crossing by the moon. I know in that moment that he was safe from spiders. That was his biggest fear in this life and it's an affliction that directly affects a lot of us—soups sorry, I am crazy fucked up right now. I don't know where the spider comment came from, much less if that statement about Sam is even true. Sometimes in death you just make shit up as a coping mechanism.

---

4   Rocky's Special is the classic steak, chicken, and shrimp special at Benihana's. You're definitely getting a rim job on the first date if the girl orders that fucking thing.

When the stout Chinaman finally stops in front of my house and pulls me out of the back of the rickshaw, he cradles my drunk body in his arms. I look up at him and muster out a belligerent sentence that I have only said one time in my entire life to another man—

"Will you stay with me?"

He nods solemnly, knowing full well that I need a Chinaman in my house to sleep that night. As he carries me up all 167 stairs, I black out at some point. The last thing I remember was pointing to Totally Fucking Mexico's gold statue and mouthing the words, "I'm going to get you a new arm." That statement was also untrue. I'd have to chop off another 5-year-old's arm and dip it in hot gold to achieve something like that, because I hate replicas. It would make me look super poor and if someone called me out, I would be embarrassed. I did however feel a sense of pride that Samantha went out the way he wanted, which was unexpected. The circumstance, not his death.

The following morning, I awake to the Chinaman sitting at the foot of my bed, arms crossed like Buddha—staring straight ahead. I immediately like this fucking guy. This is definitely someone I can screw in front of and he won't make it awkward by asking if he can join in.

"What's your name?" I ask.

"Guo," he says in a rather deep tone.

"I've never heard that name before. What the fuck does that mean?"

"A wall that surrounds a city."

"I dig that. You're kind of like my wall right now. Plus, my dick has been all over this city. How would you like to protect my dick full time? I can double the pay of whatever you were getting to play those little drums at that fuckshack?"

"Do I still have to—

"Yeah, you're definitely still going to have to watch me bone. Not because I'm into it and that's the only way I can get off or anything, it's just that I'm a spontaneous love maker and I can't guarantee when or where I'll be laying my dick down. We cool?"

"We cool," he says as he nods without ever looking back at me.

"Great. I'd shake your hand, but it appears as if I have pissed my sheets and I must go wash my whole fucking body off. Kindly wash the sheets while I bathe, please."

I stumble out of bed and into the bathroom. As I undress, Samantha's tooth falls out of my pants pocket onto the floor. I can't help but smile as I bend down to pick it up. It stinks like unprocessed meat.

"Guo, I have one more chore for you. Can you have someone sanitize this and make it into a necklace for me?"

"Sure, I have a guy."

"Great. Also, you might want to wrap this up in a napkin or something. It smells like the shit from a newborn bison after grazing for the first time. You're a peach!"

I flip it up in the air to him and he snatches it, before he begins to pull off the yellow stained sheets from my bed. Oh boy. Looks like I unleashed about three gallons into the linens. Well, that's what money is for—to pay people to do the disgusting shit you would never do in real life. Immigration is so you can pay them to do it at a lower wage. Someone has to dust the cooch of Lady Liberty.

After I clean off my nethers, I throw on a suit that would make the Squirrel Nut Zippers try and buttfuck themselves. Zoot suits were all the rage, and I'll be goddamned if I didn't have an entire closet full of them. I put in my gold horse shoe cuff links engraved **"steed"** on them, and proceed to walk my sweet ass down the stairs. I see Guo hand scrubbing my sheets in the laundry sink with an angry look on his face. Actually, I think that's just his permanent face. Him and Sam are remarkably different, but at least I never have to ask him, "What's wrong?"

"Hey Guo, you almost done with those fuck covers?"

"Five more minutes. Lot of pee," he says as he scrubs even harder.

"Great. Put them next to the rest after they're dry," I say as I point to a stack of 80 or so sets of folded sheets on a shelf behind him.

He turns and looks up, somehow managing to look even more pissed than he normally does. "What the fuck?"

"You can never have too many. Never know when an orgy is going to break out or you're going to have to escape a sudden house fire from the top floor. Anywho, when you're done I'll need a rickshaw ride to the bank and then some more quick feet over to the car dealership."

"Okay," he says resigned to the fact that this is going to be his new life.

"I'll be drinking on the the couch doing cocaine until you're ready."

"At twelve o'clock in the afternoon?"

"Is it twelve? Shit. I usually start *way* earlier. It must be Easter or something."

"No, just a regular Wednesday."

"Maybe for you, but to me each day is a gift from God—damnit wash that tooth off, Jack. The stench is rising through your pocket my man. I'm going lay down some nose cardio and try to clear my passages. Monte Cristo, bro."

Chapter 4
DON'T YOU SHINE ME UP

It felt strange being rickshawed into the bank to ask for $1.1 million in cash, mostly because I was genuinely surprised that they let me drive that fucking thing through the front doors right up to the teller. No one even blinked. I know I've said it a zillion times, but here is one more: BEING RICH IS FUCKING AWESOME.

Every single bank teller stands up straight upon my arrival and fakes a smile. The bank manager Mr. Nevins, an overweight white man in his 60's, bends a knee as if it was fine for me to fuck his wife or his daughter in front of him. The kind of money I had in this institution, I could probably fuck both at the same time. I was more respectful of these dicks than I have been in the past, because I was running an honest bidness now. Long gone were the days of me shooting the bank up, pulling my dick out, and plopping down my gold. I miss it if I'm being real with you. Instead, I'll take being rickshawed in.

"Mr. Street James, what do we owe this extreme pleasure?" Mr. Nevins says after he finally rises after bowing to me.

"Your extreme pleasure is owed to my father. His penis created me, so he deserves most of the credit."

Mr. Nevins and the rest of the tellers laugh like children on the playground in Pripyat the morning after the Chernobyl meltdown, which is to say they thought everything was fine. Turns out it wasn't, and as Guo pulls out five large empty suitcases from the back of the rickshaw, it finally dawns on them that I wasn't here to make a deposit. I was actually taking a large amount of cash from their establishment.

"I need one point one million in cash, all hundreds, and I need it put into these suitcases ASAP."

"Um, I don't know if we can do that today Mr. Street James. That's a lot of money to ask for on such short notice," Mr. Nevins says nervously.

"The way you try and sit on money, one would think it's yours. But I'm the rich man here, so you you can either give me the one point one, or I'll take the whole fifteen million out today. Your call?"

Mr. Nevins looks back at his tellers in anguish like he took a shit in his mother-in-law's guest bathroom and the flush handle broke. "Give me two hours," he finally musters out.

"Great. I'll be at the bar around the corner."

"McSorley's? Isn't it closed due to the Prohibition laws?"

I laugh and shake my head. "That tells me you aren't cool enough to be invited in. I'm going to need a grand of that cash right now if it's going to take two hours."

Mr. Nevins motions for one of the tellers to count me out a thousand. I fold it in half and tuck it in the pocket inside my sport coat as I exit. The second after I step through the front door, I rip out a key bump of coke for a little nostril sex before I get my booze on. I offer Guo some blow, but he refuses, probably sensing the day he has in store trying to look after me. As we hit the front door of McSorley's I pound his bump down for good measure.

"I'm surprised you don't get down on the North Korean nettypot?"

"No. Nothing good comes from that," he bristles.

"Actually, *everything* good comes from that. Cocaine is one of the only things on this planet that keeps me alive every day. That and booze. We're about to fix the other thing missing from my hand."

He looks at the metal door with the closed peephole. "You sure this place is open? I don't hear anyone?"

"You will," I say with a smile as I bang on the door twice.

The peephole slides open and a man with thick eyebrows and an even thicker Irish accent answers, "Yeah, what do you want?"

"A set of tits in my friend's face and some red bush in my mouth," I answer.

There's a long pause before he blurts out, "I can help you with the red bush, but you're going to have to put my cock and balls in your mouth first to get to it!"

The door opens and the entire bar erupts in laughter as the owner, Bill McSorley, bear hugs me. "Come on in you fuckers!"

It's "Japanese waterpark" packed inside. There's fifty or so drunk bastards absolutely raging in the afternoon. Guo is completely shook. I immediately throw that thousand bucks in the air and scream out—

"Drinks on me! I got two hours to kill!"

The bar erupts once again, as Bill closes the door behind me and deadbolts it. I wish I could regale you with a story on how the bar "used" to be, but thankfully it hasn't changed that much at all over the course of almost one hundred years. They never shut down once during Prohibition, they just didn't let any snitches or fuck bois in here. If you acted like an asshole, you were banished, plain and simple.

You were lucky to be there and we were lucky they were open. Most places folded out of fear. Not McSorley's, which is why I am writing my memoirs here. There's only two types of beer, light and dark. That's it. If you need more than that from a bar, chances are you're non-binary and you don't know what the fuck you want in life anyway.

I cozy up to the bar as Bill pours me a glass of dark. "Who's your friend?" He asks staring him up and down.

"He probably worked on the railroad with all your relatives."

"Get the fuck out here Saint James," Bill says as he laughs and pours himself a glass of dark as well.

Guo rolls his eyes. "I'm going to wait by the front door for the bank manager. I'll let you know when he's here."

"You want a beer, Guo?"

"No. What will your friend think if your karate instructor is drinking on the job?" He asks as he walks toward the front door.

"Nailed it, Guo." I take a swig and turn back toward Bill, "A good Chinaman is hard to find these days."

"I wouldn't know about that. We all aren't as rich as the all mighty Saint James Street James."

"True, but it doesn't seem like you're doing that bad for yourself? The place is packed. Have the feds been by?"

"Here and there, but they're not concerned about beer. They're concerned about liquor. That's what *really* gets people fucked up, so they say. They ain't had four of these though," he says as he holds up his mug.

"No, I hear you. If you do need liquor, let me know. I'm thinking about getting into business with Joe the Boss. By 'thinking', I mean I'm already doing it. So if you need a bottle of Scotch, let me know and I'll have a case sent over."

"I'm grateful to ya Street. Just be careful with Joe. Those guys play for the whole gorilla salad. They don't leave one short and curly behind neither. I'm sure I don't have to tell you that."

"No. The only thing you have to tell me is when I'm cut off. I don't even want to see the trough you're making this shit out of," I say as I hold up my mug.

"You definitely don't," he says with a laugh.

"Hey Bill, you gonna fuck him or can I get another pint down here?" A man screams out from the other end of the bar.

"I haven't made up my mind yet!" he shouts back walking over to him as the entire bar laughs.

The next two hours went exactly as you would expect. I got fucking rocked until I nearly blacked out. Mr. Nevins did come back in exactly two hours and even had the rest of his tellers load up the suitcases and put them in the rickshaw. Those motherfuckers even pulled it up in front of the bar. Sensing I was losing my footing, I slung an arm around Guo as he half-walked me out.

"It's all in and ready to go. Is that bar open?" Mr. Nevins asks.

"Not for you, hombre," I drunkenly reply.

"Oh, well, maybe you could introduce me—

"Not one fucking prayer on *this* earth or if an identical earth exists on another planet would I do that, because wouldn't be cool there either."

"Okay. One last question Mr. Street James. Can I ask what you're going to do with all that money? You know it's not insured once you leave here since it's in cash."

"No, you sure the fuck can't. You know the beauty about losing a million for someone like me? There's another fourteen more that I can blow through, so don't you worry your pretty little scroat off about it. Take me to the dealership

Guo!" I say as I fall facedown into the back of the rickshaw on top of the suitcases.

The last thing I remember is Guo's stubby little legs taking off as I passed out in the cart behind him on the way to the car dealership. There's nothing like blacking out mid-afternoon on top of a million dollars. I guess if my face were buried in a set of D tits that would be nice, but at this point, I'm just being greedy.

I wake up to Guo slapping the shit out of me in the parking lot of the Curry Chevrolet dealership on 133rd and Broadway. My peepers come to life from the glow of the dealership and I tuck down a stubborn nigh-nigh boner. I would come to know this place very well over the years. Since DUI's weren't a thing back then, I'd get rocked, wrap my car around a pole, piss on it, make a stray dog swallow the keys, then call it a night. Not once did I ever return to the vehicle the next day. Instead, I would just buy another, rinse, wash, and repeat. Them shits were only $895 a piece for a whole fucking new car, what the ass blast did I care?

Also, I *really* want to stress that cars and trucks back then were fucking awful. To me, it wasn't better than riding a horse, and most men that had cars were fucking pussies who *couldn't* ride a horse. Problem is, I couldn't keep riding horses through the streets and subject them to these loud, bullshit clown horns honking at them every fifteen feet. I had to have them out of necessity, but they really didn't get cool until the 1960's. Jay Leno can suck his own dick if he says otherwise. Pittsburgh steel workers carried tougher lunch boxes to work than these goddamn cars. The only fun in buying them was banging the women selling them.

As soon as I walk in, a male salesman in his 40's walks up. Nope. I palm his face and push him down hard across the floor. My fingers are wet from the oil his hair and my palm is sticky from the wax in his mustache. This ain't the combo, Jack. You don't approach an Alpha like this. The owner, Mr. Curry, walks over enraged as the entire dealership stops in its tracks.

"I beg your pardon, why did you shove this man?" He asks.

"Because he could be shoved. I need to see your hottest, youngest, college-aged female associate please," I say, scanning the dealership.

"I'm afraid they aren't equipped to properly sell you a car and I'm afraid I'm going to have to ask you to leave my dealership."

I spot a cute brunette in the back who has peaked her beak out from behind a wall. Her tits are perkier than the fucking *Friends* café. She spots me and bites her lower lip. Game the fuck on. Time to buy a shitty car and be a mentor to America's youth again.

"Who's the brunny with the tiger tits in the back? I want to buy a car from her."

"That's the secretary of the man you just shoved down to the ground. It's time for you to leave, sir," he says as he grabs my arm, attempting to walk me out. I flex, letting him feel my tri, and he instinctively knows I'm a powerful human who could tear his face off and wear it as my own if I wanted to.

"Here," I say as I pull out a handkerchief and throw it to the man on the ground. "Look, I know the squeaky wheel always gets the grease, but save some for the boys in the repair shop. Guo, please shut this owner the fuck up," I say motioning to this gimp.

"Sure thing," Guo says as he opens the suitcase revealing $100,000.

"So, as I was saying, I'm here to buy a car *or five*, but I'll only buy them from sweater puppets. Also, I want you to kick this man while he's on the ground."

His demeanor changes faster than Ted Bundy after he's paid the bill for a dinner date. Mr. Curry begins violently kicking his own employee like he's in a Worldstarhiphop video. Homeboy starts coughing up blood all over the white linoleum tile. Mr. Curry looks back at me like a waiter with a pepper cracker over a salad, but as per usual, I let this go past an eight count and make him ask me when to stop.

"Is this sufficient sir?" Mr. Curry asks.

"Yeah, that's fine. What's her name and what is this vehicle?" I ask as I take my index finger and run it down the entire length of the hood.

"That is—

I stuff my fingers into his mouth, silencing all of his bullshit. "I want *her* to come outside the office and tell me. Okay?"

"Bokay," he replies with my fingers still in his mouth.

"Whistle her over with my two digits."

Mr. Curry was surprising accurate without the use of his two fingers to whistle, which makes me wonder how many times he's done that or if he sucks other men's dicks on the reg. I'm not here to judge, so I remove my booger pullers from his cake hole and wipe them on the breast of his jacket. The young woman approaches me with a smile, damn near skipping across the dealership.

"Misty, this is—I'm sorry, I didn't catch your name?"

"Saint James Street James. I hate road abbreviations so I pronounce my last name."

"Nice to meet you Mr. Street James," Misty says as she extends her hand.

"I know. Why is there no ring on this hand? Do you not have a someone special in your life?"

She blushes. "No, I just finished college and I want to work on my career."

Every single man in the entire dealership erupts in laughter, including myself and Guo. The laughter comes on in waves, and lasts for more than ten minutes or so. She seems embarrassed for saying that, which she should be.

"The next thing you're going to tell us is that you want to vote?" I ask.

"Well, that sure would be nice. The Suffrage Act just passed."

She can barely get the words out before we fall on the floor laughing again. Guo is coughing like he just got done eating in a wet market back in China again. He's near complete respiratory failure. Even the salesman who got the shit kicked out of him is coughing up more of his own blood in laughter. He simply can't contain himself. Another ten minutes goes by before I'm finally able to pull myself together and stand upright.

"So, tell me about this car, Misty?" I ask like nothing happened.

"It's a Chevrolet Series 490. She goes zero to twenty in just under four minutes."

"You don't say. Four whole minutes?"

"Yeah, she's a real beauty that will impress the ladies."

"Are you impressed by this car?"

"I definitely am."

"Great. How about you take me for a spin in it? Let's see how she handles."

"Right this way," she says as she points toward the back door of the dealership.

I grab her by the arm. "Hang on. Why can't we take this one?"

"Mr. Street James, we don't test drive the showroom cars. The exact car you're looking at is out back and ready to drive," Mr. Curry interjects.

"But this is the one that *she is impressed by*. Therefore, this is the one I want to drive. Oh look, the keys are in it," I say pointing to the keys dangling from the steering wheel.

"There's simply no way to get it out of here at the moment," Mr. Curry says, refusing.

"Sure there is. Misty, hop in the car. Guo, pay the man for his window."

Guo pulls out a hundred-dollar bill and hands it to him. Mr. Curry takes it, and looks at me wondering if I'm serious. You know how this goes.

"You ready Misty? Let's see how she handles!"

Misty looks at her boss, who knows exactly what he has to let her do, but clearly isn't happy about it. Mr. Curry nods at her reluctantly as I open the driver side door for her. She hops in excitedly as I point straight ahead toward the large showroom window.

"Now Misty, I want you to drive through it like a female candidate might get elected president one day. Pretend you're driving right to the ballot box!"

Misty turns the keys and punches it, shattering the glass of the dealership as everyone looks on in shock. Tell me being rich isn't fucking rad one more time. We hit the sidewalk and jump the curb, landing safely on the street. One pedestrian was hit in the process, but they were old, so who fucking cares? Not worth my time doing research on whoever got the fender to the dome. If they were important, someone would have billed me.

Misty was smiling like two bums fucking as we drive north through the country side up to Poughkeepsie. I actually didn't say one fucking word on the way up. Don't ever ruin someone's first time driving a car unless they're heading into oncoming traffic… then obviously do something. To this day there is something wildly invigorating and care free about your first time gripping the wheel and hitting the open road.

Conversely, there is also something invigorating about gripping a girl's ass and politely boning her on the hood of a brand new car after the engine's been running for a couple hours. It's hard to express the joy in boning when the engine is still hot, not enough to burn her, but just enough to feel the heat pressing against your sack and her ass as you dig your heels into the gravel.

The family of four that was having a picnic about ten yards away underneath a tree didn't find any of that twenty-minute bone sesh enjoyable or remotely appropriate, but I stopped caring about pleasing everyone long ago. I just hoped they learned something. This was a master class in bagpiping my man. They should be lucky that they were there to witness it.

Since their two children were under the age of nine, I opted with a fourteen pump cream pie versus my standard pullout finish on the windshield to "test out the wipers on the new car." You can never really see if the wipers are working properly until they've been spunked on. Try it. You'll thank me after your next car purchase.

After shooting, I tuck my junk back in my pants and get back in the car. Misty beams from ear to ear the entire way back to the city. It's hard to remember the last time I saw someone this happy and whimsical. You could see the world of possibility in her eyes. It was uniquely genuine and real.

"This is the greatest day of my life," Misty says as she pulls up at a stop sign outside of the dealership. "Are you sure you don't want to drive? This car is actually pretty amazing."

"You keep it then. I'll buy five others," I say as I get out of the car, giving a subtle wave to Guo, who is standing behind the smashed out dealership window.

"What? You can't be serious?"

"I can be, but it just isn't that fun. Take the car and quit your job."

"I can't. Then what will I do?"

"What do you really want to do?" I say as I lean into the driver side window.

"I don't know, drink martinis and be a flapper girl at all those fancy parties I see in the papers? That seems like quite the life to me."

"Is that real?"

"Yeah, I'm never going anywhere at the dealership. It's a fucking boys club. If I get asked to pull a tire iron out of the trunk so those dirtbags can see up my skirt one more time, I'm going to bash their faces in with it."

"Whoa, whoa, whoa, you know who talks like that? Serial killers. Rapists. Vegans. People who ride in wheelchairs with just one wheel. You're better than that, Misty."

"Says who?"

"Says me. And I know what I'm talking about. Look, you waited more than two whole hours to have sex with me. No woman does that. With any other girl, I'm usually up in those pork chop piss flaps in under an hour, but you played hard to get."

"I was driving the whole time so—

"Sssshhhh," I say as I put my index finger to her lips shutting her the fuck up. "And now you're going to drive this car home and start that new life you were talking about. Throw on your best flapper dress and come to my party tonight. It's going to be electric. Here's my card."

I reach into my pocket and hand her a card that reads: **"You know who the fuck I am. Quit playing baby games. You're not a baby. I would never give my card to a baby. They can't read this shit. I'm looking right at you and I can clearly see you're not a baby."** My address was written in small print at the bottom. She looks up at me and smiles.

"Thank you. I'll be there."

"I know you will," I say as I smile and tap the hood of the car before crossing the street.

"Saint James?"

"Yeah?" I say looking back at her as I reach the front steps of the dealership. She gives the car a little gas to catch up.

"This really has been the best day of my life—

Wham!

A car coming from the other direction slams into Misty, killing her on impact. The cross street she was rolling through didn't have a stop sign and she apparently didn't look both ways. The other driver died too along with his wife and what appears to be three small children. Women *shouldn't* really drive. RIP Misty. Mr. Curry and Guo look at me in shock, still standing where the dealership window used to be.

"So, obviously I don't want *that* car, but I'll take five others in that model. To be honest, they don't appear to be very safe, so you should probably throw me a deal or something. Just saying."

Chapter 5
THIS MOB SHIT IS FUN

A t exactly 8am sharp the next morning, I hear a rap at the front door as I sit on the couch sipping coffee with a shot of whiskey. I wipe my eyes and motion for Guo to answer the door. The young kid, Al Capone, whose life I saved, takes his news boy cap off as he enters my home. Guo hands him the suitcase with one million dollars in it. Al looks at it, then at me, before clearing his throat.

"You look like a nervous kid asking a prostitute for a rimmer."

"Well, Mr. Street James—it's just," he stutters.

"What? Speak up for fuck sakes man!"

"My boss, Joe, he wants me to count it. This is the first time you guys are doing business together and all. Sorry, this is awkward for me as well," he says, barely able to make eye contact.

"Not a problem. But since I haven't gone to bed yet, and you're going to keep me up another hour or two while you count this bullshit, let's make it a little more awkward."

"You haven't gone to sleep—

I put my fingers in my mouth and loudly whistle, soliciting two blonde, buck naked prostitutes I was boning last night from the other room. They're not wearing a stitch of clothing, and both are as equally hungover as me. The taller one bends down and crushes a line off the coffee table like an ace of spades.

"You good with this Capone? That way they can't hide any money either. Spin around ladies."

The girls spin around in a full circle with their hands up. "Mr. Street James, this isn't necessary," he says flabbergasted.

"No, it is. Girls, do eighty jumping jacks so he can see that you aren't hiding any money in your sphincters or meat wallets."

As the girls begin to jump he protests, "Please stop. I'll take your word for it. They're good."

I stand up. "No. Apparently they aren't, and I'm not since you're not taking my word that all the money is there. When they stop at eighty, I want you to count out the money with them. The full fucking million."

"But I just—

"Nope. I don't even want to re-fuck them now. I'm going to bed. Guo will see you out when you're done."

I drink the remainder of my whiskey and splash of coffee, pound a rail of murder snow off the coffee table, and throw my mug into the fire place shattering it into pieces before walking up the stairs. This begins the longest bender I have ever been in my life, for no reason other than I could.

Plus, the two hot blondes only add to the legend when he goes back and tells the boys what happened over at Saint James Street James place this morning.

"Ah, Mr. Street James?"

"Jesus fucking Christ, what?" I say turning around pissed.

"Are all those brand new cars out front yours?" Capone asks.

"Yeah, why?"

"Well, Joe usually likes his associates to keep a low profile. Someone pulls up with five brand new cars, people get suspicious is all."

"Look around you? You're in a penthouse brownstone with two dime pieces wearing nothing but what the good lord gave them as they count out a million dollars in cash next to a pile of some of the finest coke in the world. It's not exactly like you're meeting me in the back alley behind *Ray's Famous Pizza* and I'm shooting dice to make rent on a one bedroom in Hell's Kitchen. I AM ACTUALLY FUCKING RICH. I could walk outside and take a shit in those cars in front of the police chief, tell him I bought them simply to serve as outhouses, and there's not a goddamn thing he could do. Goodnight Capone," I say as I make my way up the stairs.

"Goodnight," he says.

"After you deliver that to your boss, bring me my booze for tonight. Got it?"

"Yes sir," he says as I double bird him behind my back and keep walking.

It was difficult to sleep, and I lay in my bed staring at the ceiling, brainstorming about the party I was going to throw that night. It had to be a spectacle, otherwise it would be just another bash in a long line of parties at the Saint James house. This one had to be special. Unforgettable. Women needed to get pregnant *and* crown at this party. It was hard to think.

To say I was "wired" right now would be an understatement. Coffee and coke before bedtime was a recipe for disaster, especially for someone who doesn't sleep that much anyway. I count along with the girls as they entered the "70's" phase of their jumping jacks downstairs. They were out of breath and I can hear their tits slapping against their rib cages as they close in on 80. That sound is as so distinct and hearing it in unison is like hearing Phil Spector's *Wall Of Sound* for the first time. I suddenly find the inspiration and know what I have to do. I get up and run over to the stairwell, obviously still buck naked, and call down to Guo.

"I need you to go buy me all the Olympic equipment you possibly can for the party tonight. Find something from every sport. I'm going to evac my bowels into the toilet and then probably pass out in the bathtub afterward. Coffee and coke, amiright?"

"Are you serious boss?" Guo replied.

"Yes to all of the above that I just said. Also, I need engraved invitations stating that everyone must wear athletic attire. You're all invited tonight too, ladies."

The girls clap excitedly as I sprint toward the bathroom. My cheeks barely kissed the seat before the first volcanic blast. Whoopsie ding-dong. Coffee this late was a terrible idea. My legs kick up like a little kid at a Mexican Birthday party getting thrown on top of a Shetland pony for the first time. I stare straight ahead at a Greek statue of a nude man throwing a discus, which is the centerpiece of my generous master bathroom.

"Guo! I also need 100 pounds of clay! Don't fuck me!" I scream out as the next blast hits the toilet. Straight Vesuvius down there.

Around 8pm that evening, the guests arrive wearing track uniforms, wrestling singlets, tennis skirts, etc.—all of them having no idea what they are in store for. As everyone is drinking dirty martinis and glad handing cocktail wieners, an older British gentleman I hired walks down the long staircase and stops halfway down. He blows into his trumpet and a man in his 20's jogs up to the front door and into the living room holding a lit torch, placing it in the good arm of Totally Fucking Mexico's gold statue.

After the torch was secure he calls out, "Let the games begin," before jogging off through the partygoers out the back door.

"Here ye! Here ye! Ladies and gentlemen, I give you our Olympic Committee host for the evening, Mr. Saint James Street James!" the British man exclaims.

All the partygoers turn and look around the room trying to find my entrance. Little did they know I was in the middle of them, nude and covered in clay, exactly like the Greek statue in my bathroom. I twist and turn, breaking free from the hundred pounds of wet clay I had Guo apply to my body in the bath tub. The place erupts as I shake off some dried clay from around my eyes, before grabbing a drink off the waitress tray.

Raising it toward the crowd I shout, "I know the 1920 Olympic Games in Belgium aren't until August, so how about we hold them on American soil tonight? Each room is dedicated to a different sport where men and women are encouraged to go head to head with one another if they choose. For example, this room is dedicated to wrestling, and clothing is optional for either gender."

A rich white man in his 40's raises his hand. "What if we just want to have sex in there and not engage in the act of wrestling?"

"There's still a winner and loser if you know what I mean, so I'll allow it. A victor must be declared. Wink." This elicits laughter from the party as I walk over to the next room. "Now this room is dedicated to 'tug of war'… except we aren't using any rope."

The rich white man perks up again. "So, we're just using our penises?"

"Yes, that's correct."

"Brilliant! I always wanted my penis tugged unbelievably hard and now that day is here!"

"Try and keep it together man. The swimming and water polo events will take place in the bathtub upstairs, and the roof of my house has been converted into an ice rink for hockey."

The rich white man raises his hand once more. "All penises again?"

"Yes goddamnit. Now fencing, still penises, will be held downstairs in the room to the right, and all track and field events will be held in the living room—including javelin."

"Where do we throw the javelins?" Another rich white male in his 40's asks.

"Please throw the javelins into the Van Gogh painting you see above the fireplace. I fucking hate that guy and his work is shit. The only reason I bought it was to use as a reminder to not cut my fucking ear off when I get high."

"Smart. I learned that lesson the hard way," another man says as he tilts his head back revealing his missing left ear.

"Sorry about that, chief. Now, only *gold* medals will be awarded for each event, because I'm not fucking poor. You want silver or bronze, go rip out a hobo's tooth. I don't do that shit here. The winners will join me in the master bedroom for a classic Greek orgy. May the best athletes win."

The room erupts into applause as Guo holds up a starter gun and fires it into the air. Partygoers immediately stagger into the different rooms that fit their skillset. Homeboy who just asked that last question, takes off his pants and greases up his dong before quickly entering the "Tug room." Good for him. This is what it's all about.

Also, I'm aware that every person at the party was described as "rich and white." It was New York in the 1920's, if you could afford to live in the city, chances are you were white. If you're currently offended by real life history, go watch a new reboot of an 80's flick where they threw a trans in there to make the cast more diverse. That should make you feel better.

I reach down and pick up a shot put and throw it through a fucking window out into the street. It caves in the hood of one of my five cars and I share a good chuckle with a married woman with huge tits who I'm definitely boning later. Guo shakes his head as he looks out the window at the car. I flash him a five sign with my fingers like I'm Kobe Bryant jumping on the scorer's table after his fifth title. Again, those cars I bought were fucking garbage. They deserved to be treated as such.

The shot-put incident really ramped up the party though. It let everyone know that *anything* goes tonight, which is important. When the host wrecks his own house, it makes everyone feel like they can destroy shit too and they can throw all their inhibitions away. I knew the statement I was making and that's why I'm the fucking best. To say shit got out of hand tonight would be an understatement. It. Got. Bug. Fuck. Son.

The first three dudes in the hundred-yard dash rip insane lines of coke and then run right through the fucking wall and into the kitchen. I had recently contemplated opening it up for a more "homey" feel and this just saved me a GC. The three men walk out back through the hole in dry wall laughing all the way to the bar as they dust each other off. We pound shots and exchange business cards, before I hear a scream downstairs that I need to tend to. Guo rushes over to me.

"You want me to go down there boss?" He asks.

"No, I know the type of scream that is," I say with a laugh.

"You do?"

"This isn't the first party I've thrown, Guo. Politely and *discreetly* ask if anyone is a doctor and have them meet me downstairs, okay?"

"Sure thing, boss."

I grab another martini off of a waitress' tray and grab her by the pussy, because you really did use to be able to do that shit back then, so why wouldn't you? As I casually stroll down the stairs sniffing my fingers, I walk toward the room where the screaming has now become more muffled. I can hear a man arguing with a woman as I lean in against the door. As I turn the door handle, I am immediately greeted by one of the more surprising things I've seen in my life. A man in his 50's is bent over on all fours with half of a wooden tennis racket in his ass.

"I'm going to have to pull it out or the pain won't stop," an attractive woman in her 30's says.

"It'll prolapse Rita! You have to go slow!" he shouts back at her.

"It's not like I was just going to rip it out like I was trying to pull it out of a hornet's nest, Carl."

I clear my throat loudly announcing my presence. "As IOC Chairman, I'm obligated to ask what went on in here."

The man on all fours looks up at me, "Mixed doubles. I dove for a drop shot and fell asshole down on to my partner's racket. Simple mistake."

"Of course. And where is the team you are playing?"

"They're in the closet having sex. They got bored during the injury timeout," the man says with a shrug.

"Understandable. Well look, I'm no doctor, but one is on the way—

Guo suddenly grabs my arm before motioning to an older gentleman in his 70's, standing over my shoulder, who's completely buck naked wearing a stethoscope. "Here is the doctor you requested, boss."

I look at him and shake my head. "I don't think you'll be needing that stethoscope tonight, Doc. This is strictly anal."

"It's for me actually. I almost gave myself a heart attack in the high jump on to the bed upstairs, but I cleared four feet," he says proudly.

"Good for you. If you could pull this racket out of this man's anus that would be swell. We have four other people waiting to play."

"You got it. Any stock tips for the market?"

"Oil is going to be up," I say as I point to the man's ass. Everyone laughs like nothing is going on and this dude totally doesn't have half a racket sticking out of his ass.

Guo whispers into my ear. "Boss we got another problem in your master bathroom upstairs."

"Water polo?"

"Synchronized swimming event," he says with his head down.

"How bad can it be?"

"It's bad, boss."

"Okay. Lead the way," I say to him as we walk out of the room. Just before we leave, I turn back to to the man on the floor. "Wash that racket off in the sink after you pull it out, alright? People will be using it afterward, so show some respect for the game."

"Will do, sir. Thanks," the man says as he waves with one arm.

I follow Guo up the stairs into the master bathroom where I see a four-piece orchestra playing around my enormous bath tub scoring a synchronized swimming event in full progress. Six nude women swim with precision, executing leg kicks in the air as their torsos are underwater. One girl is submerged between them in the middle, seemingly used as spotter or distancing device. Clearly they've worked on this routine before, or had some form of rehearsal. About eight to ten other people are also in the room enjoying this act of showmanship as well. I lean over to Guo and whisper, not wanting to ruin their performance.

"This is impressive. Everyone is in unison. They're not even a tenth of a second off. I don't see what the problem is, Guo?

"Boss, you see the girl in the middle floating"

"Yeah, so?"

"She's dead," he says.

I look more closely, and yes— she is definitely just floating at the surface, face down and she does appear to be dead.

I lean back over to Guo. "From my perspective, I don't see the problem *right* now. Obviously later, of course, we're going to have some naysayers who might be upset. But in my experience, it's always better to ask for forgiveness."

He looks at me confused. "What? Shouldn't we stop this?"

"God no. There's nothing we can do for her now and these ladies are giving the performance of their life out here tonight. Shit, come to think of it, maybe they are doing it *for* her. Who are we to stop what appears to be a perfect routine?"

"So what do you want me to do?" he asks.

"Wait for them to finish, applaud like a gentleman, then roll her up in the carpet and dump the body out back in the dumpster when everybody exits the tub. Or, prop her up in my room in a chair, throw some sunnies on her, and she can watch me screw her teammates afterward. I almost feel bad for leaving her out. Obviously, I don't want her staying in here after I fall asleep, so use your discretion on what would be the best time to dispose of the body. I just don't want to see it."

"This is fucked up, boss."

"Well so is life, but we come back out of it on the other side hoping to learn from it and that's what makes you do more drugs. Speaking of which, go downstairs and grab me some. I'm going to stay and watch the rest of this routine."

I sit down on an ottoman and fire up a heater, while the others start getting misty-eyed watching this eleven-minute masterpiece. As the Hamptons Six (yeah I gave them a nickname because these women were that special) leapt out of the water, everyone cheered and gave them a thunderous applause. I got caught up in the moment and even got a little choked up myself from all the raw energy in the room. The women took their cue like the professionals they were and held hands in the tub, taking a unified bow. Together. As a team... *except for the dead one.*

"I don't need to see anymore. I'm ready to declare you the gold medalists in synchronized swimming. I've never seen anything quite like this. You girls left it all in the water. Especially her," I say as I point at the deceased.

"Thank you!" One of them shouts out excitedly as the others begin to hug one another and fist pump, each of them taking their accomplishment in.

"Guo, the medals please?" I ask as I snap my fingers.

He hands me five gold medals, shaking his head. "Here you go."

I look down at my hand and count them, before cocking my head. "I'm going to need one more boss man."

"What? No, please don't do this," he says under his breath as he pleads with me with his eyes.

"She earned it just as much as any girl out here tonight. Give me the medal. I'll place it on her."

"This is taking it too far—

"No, I'm respecting the fallen. My only hope is that you'd do it for me one day, Guo. But based on your not so subtle judgment, I highly fucking doubt it. I'm also going to need that cocaine I asked for."

Guo reluctantly reaches into his pocket and pulls out the extra gold medal, while handing me the bag of coke in the process. I pat him on the shoulder and mouth the words, "You did the right thing." He definitely didn't, but I was so fucked up that I thought the tribute seemed appropriate, so I did it anyway. In no way, shape, or form am I proud of what transpired next—but it did, and that's on me.

That's when I decide to climb inside my enormous bathtub and place a gold medal around each of their necks individually, as well as opting for the European double kiss on each cheek afterward. Then I lean down and wrap the last remaining medal around the dead girl's neck. It was so heavy that it pulled her down under water a few more inches further.

Suddenly, I could feel the warm water between my toes—and something came over me—I wanted to be part of this moment. Fucking drugs, man.

You know when your team wins the big rivalry game and you rush the field afterward because deep down you're so excited that you just want to be part of it? That's what happened to me in this moment with the Hamptons Six. I wanted to be with them. Right here. Right now. In this water, which was *their* water. So, I grab a handful of cocaine and throw it against the bare wet chest of the girl with the biggest tits and motor-boated them shits until my face was whiter than a street mime.

"Let's have a fucking orgy!"

"Yeah!" everyone in the master bathroom screams out.

One by one everyone takes off their clothes, hops into the bathtub, and starts fucking. That's how amped everyone was. The numbers worked out evenly too, which *never* happens in an orgy. What are the chances? I obviously saddle up with the big titted girl, you know SJSJ at this point I should hope. If I want bee stings, I'll go stick my hand inside a tree cavity.

As I look around at the others, all I keep thinking is, this had to be what it was like in Greece during the first games in the 8th Century. I'm just happy I can do my part to help recreate some of that history. What the fuck am I saying? Again, I am zooted right now, brother. I *really* can't stress that enough.

What I do know is this many people fucking in a huge bath tub for that length of time creates a lot of water rising up over edge and spilling onto the floor. With everyone paired off around the sides of the tub, the dead girl kind of drifts back and forth, depending on which couple was fucking the hardest. I felt her head bump up against my leg a few times during intercourse, but I blocked it out. If she could give it her all, this is the least I can do. On the inside, I could sense something bigger was about to happen.

"Alright, on the count of of six, let's all orgasm together in honor of what we just witnessed in here tonight, okay?"

"Let's do it!" a man screamed out.

"No one pull out either! One, two, three, four, five, six—Ohhhhhhh fuck!!!"

I feel the floor in the bathroom give way and the eleven of us in the tub come crashing down through the ceiling. The gigantic tub shatters all over the living room floor, sending bodies flying. I was still able to cum, but it wasn't what I had hoped for. Luckily, the starter gun hadn't gone off for the next 100-meter relay, so no one got crushed to death under the weight of the tub downstairs. Just as I try to regain my senses, the cops burst through the door with their guns drawn.

"Everybody freeze—what the fuck?" A police officer says with a thick New York accent.

He stands at the front door in utter shock. The way the bodies hit the ground, the naked dead girl lands in the middle of the living room alone face down, proudly wearing her gold medal. There was still so many drunken, nude people running around screaming still trying to complete their events. The police officer looks at the multiple javelins thrown into the Van Gogh over the fireplace.

"Who's responsible for all of this?"

"She is," a man's voice pipes up as he walks up from downstairs. "I'm sorry to hold everyone up, but it took Rita an hour before she was finally able to remove the tennis racket from my anus. Who's up next in mixed doubles?"

"Jesus Christ!" Rita screams as the cops point their guns at them.

"Real guns or starter guns?" The man asks.

"Real guns, real cops. Hands up, sport," the cop says.

"Okay, take it easy," he says as he raises his hands.

He slowly drops his racket and as it hits the floor, we can see a small nickel size nugget of poop dangling off the end. The way the end of the racket ricochets, it pops back up off the marble floor and flies through the air in slow motion. It's completely silent and every eye in the room is now focused on this small piece of feces drifting through the night air. Four seconds later, it lands perfectly on the toe of the cop's freshly polished shoe. He's redder than an Irishman's nose in his mid 50's.

"Somebody is going to fucking jail tonight," the officer says as he looks at me.

"Understood," I say as I get up off the floor.

"Is that girl dead?" He asks in shock.

"Yes, she is deceased. Natural causes, but she died a hero as you can see. You ready?" I say as Guo hands me a pair of pants and a collared shirt to put on.

"Let's go. You rich people are some sick fuckers," he says shaking his head as he escorts me out. That statement remains true for every rich man to this very day.

Chapter 6
LET'S HAVE A SIT DOWN

Downtown New York City jails are exactly what you see in old television shows, except the smell of urine is more powerful than you can imagine. Cops love to give you the old "you get to piss one time when I say" routine in lockup. When you're in the hoosegow—obviously you have your own shitter—but when you're in downtown holding cells, you have to ask to piss. Here's the thing, ninety percent of the people in here are drunk as shit. There ain't nobody asking twice, so the floor becomes the Danang River. Police are the ones that have to clean it up, so I was always surprised they weren't that cool when you asked. Tonight, someone is grabbing an extra mop and a pair of waders after what I unleashed. I was interrupted by the cop banging on my cell door after my third shake.

"Hey, Saint James, knock it the fuck off!"

"Ain't nowhere else to spend the morning gold, so the floor will have to do. You charging me with anything? Cause if not, I give myself another fifteen tops before you're all wearing lifejackets. I had quite a few tonight."

"Speaking of which, where did you get the booze? You tell me that and you'll be back pissing in the comfort of your own home in no time."

"But your place is better suited. I'll wait for my lawyer before we rap about life and our trials and tribulations," I say as I stuff my dick back into to my pants and take a seat on the bench in my cell.

"Have it your way, asshole."

"That's the same thing that man said to that tennis racket before it was inserted," I say pointing down at his shoes.

"Fuck you," he says as I light up a heater and laugh as he storms off.

First of all, I'm not a snitch. Never have, never will. I'd rather have my head sewn to a carpet full of dirt with a thousand *Roombas* set on "high" than to snitch on people. That's me as a person though. The only things I hold dear to me is my dick, my gun, and my word. If I'm holding coke it's usually gone by the end of the night, but the other three are always with me *guaranteed.*

I'm also sure as fuck not snitching on Joe The Boss. As hard as I am, I'm not foolish enough to think I can outgun the mob in New York City. There's too many stairwells, speakeasy's, and dimly lit alley's—they'll get you eventually. Plus, I didn't want to hide, I love it here. I'll take that bid like a goddamn man and make the best of it rather than look over my shoulder like a fat man shamefully grabbing a bag of Cool Ranch Doritos out of the pantry at 2am with his wife sleeping upstairs.

When you're rich in New York, you want to enjoy the fuck out of it. To be real, I knew the mob was probably worried. Behind every cool mob story from back in the day, is another story followed by someone who had snitched on them. To them, I'm just a dude who dropped off a million in cash and got arrested the same night. The only thing they know about me is that I threw a man into a wood chipper. Twice. That's it. I assume they'll be sending their own lawyer any second so I don't—

"Saint James, don't say a fucking word! These cock-suckers will arrest an innocent man molesting a street mime in a second!" a man screams in an Italian accent.

Right on cue, my "new" lawyer "Slim" Danny Denunzio, who weighed close to 400 pounds, huffs through the station barreling toward my holding cell. The cop who arrested me and a few other officers hanging around his desk look pissed, which means they obviously know him. Their looks tell me I'll be out of here pretty quickly. Danny motions toward my cell and twirls his index finger in their faces.

"I want to talk to my client," he blurts out.

"Is he a new client Danny, I ain't never seen him around you guys?" The cop replies.

"You can't see anyone around me, John."

"Not if you keep eating those sandwiches," he says motioning towards a fresh sub that rests underneath Danny's arm.

"Late night snack. Now let me see my client. Give us five and then you can question him, okay?"

The cop shakes his head and reluctantly lets him by as he makes his way to back to me. By the way, I ended up loving this fucking guy over the years. I would end up needing him *a lot.* He loved to make the cops feel as uncomfortable as he possibly could, so he always showed up with a party sub from the local deli in his neighborhood. I'm talking a whole six footer, except it was for himself.

"You talk to them about anything?" Danny whispered through the bars.

"Not a chance. They don't even know my middle name," I say as I get up off the bench in my cell.

"Good. What is your middle name by the way?"

"I don't have one."

"Even better," he smiles. "Do me a favor, whatever question they ask you, wait until I finish my sandwich, then answer something completely nonsensical. We'll be out of here in a half hour. Got it?"

"Yup."

"Good. We're ready when you are boys!" he screams back toward the cops.

They unlock the cell and walk me down to the interrogation room. Danny lays down his sandwich on the desk and opens up a brief case with hundreds of papers stuffed into it, which had nothing do with my case what-so-ever. All of it was a distraction designed to frustrate and humiliate the cops at all costs. It was masterful to watch. Even I got so fucking caught up in his whole shit, that I felt nervous watching him. He'd shuffle papers, write on a few, then stuff others back into the briefcase. It was maddening to be in an isolated room with him.

"Okay boys, fire away. You can ask anything you want," he said as he finally sat still and folded his hands for the first time.

"Who do you work for Saint James? Just give me the name of the guy who gave you the booze?"

"I hate to do this fellas, but before you answer that, you mind if I have a quick bite? My old lady threw me out a couple months ago and I haven't had a decent meal since."

The cops exhale in unison, knowing what's coming. "Sure. By all means, go ahead."

They knew they didn't have a choice and Danny was going to do it anyway, so they let him eat his sandwich. Danny's go-to move is that he would wait until the very first question was asked during the interrogation, then slowly unwrap the six-foot sandwich and eat the entire fucking thing in front of them before letting his client answer a single question. It took him twenty-five fucking minutes to eat that goddamn thing. It was equal parts mesmerizing and disgusting, but he was the greatest lawyer ever. The second he finished his sub, he holds up his index finger, slowly licking the remaining remnants off his other fingers, then asks the police in his thick accent—

"I'm sorry, could you repeat the question again?"

Audible gasps echo off the walls of the interrogation room from the policemen. The beauty of it is, Danny wasn't even Italian. He just faked the accent for business, or maybe just to fuck with the cops? No one *really* knew. I never got an actual answer and I also never fucking cared. There's just some people who are so delightfully odd in this life that you just kind of go with it.

You know these people. They're not actually friends, and you've never spent any time with them outside of a dinner function or anything—but when you see them—you feel like you know exactly where they've been so there's no need to ask them the question. Slim Danny was doing coke off a low rent prosty on 53rd, and you could smell every last scent of her pussy in his moustache. Yeah, of course he's the type of dude who goes down on hookers. Like I said, *you know exactly where he's been.*

The cop was already exhausted by the time he could ask his first question again, "Who do you work for Saint James? Where did you get the booze? We'll let you go if you tell us and that will be it. We won't come looking for you again. Just answer this one simple question."

Danny puts his hand on my knee and nods. "Go ahead. You can tell them, it's okay," he says in his horrific Italian accent.

I look at Danny and shrug my shoulders sheepishly, then lean in closer to the cops. They seemed genuinely surprised, so they lean forward into to me. I take a deep breath, lick my lips like Roger Clemens at a Senate hearing, and blink my eyes a few times. I can't believe I was actually about to do this, but I blurt out in a full on deaf accent, "Nasier Wook White."

"What did you say? Nasier Wook White?" The cop asks.

"Yeah, Nasier Wook White," I say again in a deaf accent.

Slim Danny nods at me and smiles like a proud parent of a child crossing the finish line in the Special Olympics. Sorry for that one. Not really. He then looks at the cops.

"He's saying, 'not sure what they look like'. I'm sorry boys, my client goes deaf every Wednesday. It's a rare condition caused by an AM radio frequency that used to penetrate his dog as a child. I guess it rubbed off on him. Is there anyone in here that could possibly sign to him, or has at least spent one year on some sort of high school or college flag team? Otherwise, he's not going to be able to continue."

The cops are pissed. "Oh, so you're fucking deaf now? I bet you'll be able to hear the cell door shut behind you just fine when we put you in prison. We'll find out who your boss is with or without you. But if it's without you, we can't help you. Think about it."

"So, are you charging my client with anything or can I go back to going down on a prostitute?" Slim Danny asks as he runs his fingers through his sweet stache.

The cops look at one another and shake their head. "We'd fine you for the booze, but you can certainly pay it, so there's no point. Keep throwing your little parties. We'll be back."

I sign to him the "sunset" motion by closing my right arm down on top of the other, before walking out. This is the first time I've been pulled in by the cops here, so naturally I had a lot of questions. Slim Danny knew this, and he yanks me into a restroom stall before leaving the station. He pulls a white baggy out of the pocket in his sport coat filled with cocaine and dumps it on top of the tank of the toilet, immediately crushing rails.

"First time?" He asks after ingesting a huge gator tail.

"Yes," I say as I partake in a rail.

"Well, the good thing is, you didn't rat. This will get back to Joe The Boss and you will remain in good graces. Chances are one of them is on his payroll and they already made the call to him when we left."

"Can I still throw parties? This has become a major part of my livelihood and I don't want to fuck this up."

Danny crushes yet another epic rail off the toilet. "Yeah man, you're fine. Just hire extra security at the door, a staff to hide the booze in case they fight their way in, and for Christ sakes—don't let any girls drown to death during fake Olympic

Games inside your house. And if they do, call me and we'll get rid of them. Got it?"

"I can do that."

"Great. It'll all be fine, baby. I'm going to go find that prostitute to go back down on. These girls love it, baby."

"That's totally not true."

"One more for the road," he says blasting down another line. "You keep the rest and I'll bill you for it. Oh and just so you know, the boss wants to see you for dinner tomorrow night. He'll send someone to grab you. In the meantime, I'll tell him you didn't say shit."

He crushes his last rail, slaps me on the shoulder, and barely squeezes his way out past me through the bathroom stall. Slim Danny had places to be at 6am, but I didn't. I needed to sleep and consider the severity of what had just happened to me... *obviously after I finished off the rest of his coke.*

As I walk through the streets on the way back to my place, I notice a homeless group of black men playing saxophone around a barrel of fire. Naturally, I tell them how much they suck, grab one of their saxes, and play a proper tune for them to learn so hopefully they would stop being homeless. I pooch one of their last bottles of wine and consider it payment for my lesson before walking away. They probably wanted me to have it, so I did.

The following evening Al Capone came to my door at approximately 7:30pm to pick me up for an 8 o'clock dinner.

These fucks are prompt, I'll give them that. Guo hands me my coat at the front door and my shoulder holster already loaded up with my pistols. This move was pretty standard for me back then, even though I wasn't expecting anything heavy to go down. He puts my jacket over my shoulders and I ease into it.

"You want me to go with you boss?" Guo asks.

"No, I'm good. The kid can take me. Where are we going tonight? A Mexican restaurant?"

Capone bursts out laughing. "No sir. You're definitely having Italian tonight, and probably every other night."

"What's the name of the joint?"

"Barbetta's. It's over on 46th Street. Real nice place."

"I'm so fucking hungry that I'd eat at a buffet inside a whore house right about now. See you soon, Guo. Enjoy a night off after you finish shining my sixty-six pairs of shoes, will you? You're too stressed for no reason."

"No, there's definitely a reason," he says as he points to the gigantic hole in the ceiling where the tub came crashing through.

"Goddamnit I'm awesome. I forgot about that. Obviously fix that too. I'll see you later fuckface."

Door to door, it was fifteen minutes, and let me tell you Barbetta's was worth it. I notice the gorgeous interior right away. Mostly because there was an old fat Italian woman named Carmella standing at the hostess stand screaming—

"GORGEOUS INTERIOR ISN'T IT?"

"It's even more beautiful when you scream it that loud to accentuate it. Never be afraid to be *too* loud. Men love women who are really loud."

"What do you want from, I'm Italian?" Carmella says with a hearty laugh.

I've always hated that fucking phrase. It's been around since these motherfuckers stepped off the goddamn boat. Being a rude, loud, asshole isn't going to be excused by you pointing it out. It's like black people who scream at the the movie screen during a film and when you look back at them they say, "I PAID FOR THIS TICKET LIKE EVERYBODY ELSE." Cool. I haven't washed my dick since I fucked that chick in my tub next to that floating dead girl, but I'm not going to announce that to complete strangers just because I can.

"Joe is waiting for you over here," she says as she points.

"You mean the only table that has actual people in it in the whole entire place?"

"That's the one. Follow me, hon."

Joe stands up and kisses both of my cheeks, before instructing his four bodyguards with him at the table to pat me down. Capone looks on nervously as I politely raise my hands skyward. The guards open up my coat, exposing my two pistols peeking out of my shoulder holster. He waves them off and gives them a wink.

"We're good," he says.

"You sure, boss," one of the bodyguards says begrudgingly.

"Everything is fine. We're going to have a nice meal. Please," he says as he waves them off again. "Have a seat Mr. Street James."

"Thank you," I say as I take off my jacket, placing it on the back of my chair. "How are the breadsticks here? Are they never ending?"

Joe laughs. "What do you mean?"

"I don't know, I figure a place like this, they must have never ending breadsticks. The woman at the front treated me like family."

"Well, that's because you are now. I heard you didn't snitch."

"Not my style. My style is to—

"Completely fuck up everything in your path and party? Yeah. I heard about your little shindig last night."

"She deserved the medal Joe, and I for goddamn sure wasn't going to take it away from her."

"I don't give a shit about the gold medal. I give a shit about your profile. It's too high and it raises too many questions. And right now you're not doing yourself, or us, any favors by purchasing five cars and holding mock Olympic games with some of New York's finest in your living room.

We don't operate like that."

"Well, what can I say? I do. I have the money to back it up and I'll never say a word about where the booze comes from. Plus, it takes some of heat off you. I bet nobody hassled you or any of your guys last night, because every cop was focused on my place. Am I right?"

He nods his head in agreement. "No, there were no complaints from my guys about the police giving them a hard time last night."

"Good. Now what do you recommend for two straight males eating in an empty restaurant all alone together?"

"The bolognaise. It's the best I've had since the old country."

"Greece? Greece is the old country, right?"

He roars with laughter, "Get the fuck out of here!"

As I go to put the menu down, I spot seven guys in trench coats walk through the front door with Tommy guns. The first one in blows the hostess Carmella away, riddling her chest with bullets as the other six men unleash on Joe's four bodyguards. I leap across the table toppling Joe backward off his chair while simultaneously grabbing Capone with my right arm pulling him down with me. The bodyguards begin trading gunfire with the men distracting them just long enough for me to toss the table upright so Joe and Capone are protected momentarily. I pull my six shooters out of my shoulder holsters as I look over to them.

"Stay down."

Capone nods and pulls a handgun out of a calf holster. The look of that scared kid in the warehouse is gone now, and has been replaced by that of a stone cold killer. I motion for him to go right as the bodies of Joe's four bodyguards hit the ground next to us, lifeless. It's now or never, because this wooden table ain't stopping .45 caliber Thompson submachine guns from piercing our fucking suits.

"Now," I say as I spin left.

Capone and I rise in unison and begin firing. By now you've read the other two books and you know daddy is amidex and only going for headshots. I take out four of them in spectacular fashion while Capone ices the other two as we turn this place into a blood soaked wet t-shirt contest. From behind us we hear gunshots and see two more men entering through the kitchen. They kill the cooks and the busboys instantly. The problem for them is that there's only one point of entry into the dining room, which is through the kitchen door. I look at Capone and smile as he tries to contain his laughter. They have no idea that the carnage in here is their hombres, not ours.

They have a good 15 to 20 second walk until they get to us while we wait on them. That's when I feel the crotch in my pants rise eight inches. I was getting a murder boner. It's better than any sexual boner you can ever experience, obviously because you're about to murder someone. God-damnit it's the fucking best. There is no pill, cream, or pros-titute that can recreate that kind of boner and you only know what it feels like if you've murdered in the past. It's a wave that overtakes your entire body moments before you're about to remove their soul from this earth. Ask anyone who has had one, it makes everything else in this world seem dull. Only drugs and alcohol can moderately get you anywhere near that level, hence I do both daily.

As the two men stroll through the kitchen entrance, Capone and I light them up faster than a Karen calling for a manager when her potato skins arrive *with* her salad. It's called an "appetizer" for a reason. The look of shock on these men's faces is priceless. So was the blood coursing through my boner. If you could extract that blood and inject it, humans would live forever. That's how fucking powerful it is.

I help Joe the Boss up off the floor and he dusts himself off. Looking around the restaurant, bodies are strewn out everywhere. It's a fucking massacre. The three of us are the only ones alive. I put the table that we were hiding behind down on all four legs again and pick up two chairs. Joe looks at me strange.

"What the fuck are you doing?"

"I'm hungry. Capone said we were having dinner tonight."

"The fucking place is shot to shit and everyone is dead, pal."

"Did it ruin your appetite? Because it sure as shit didn't ruin mine. It's not like you fucking did anything."

Joe smirks at me. "I'll play along. Who's going to cook for us? The chef is fucking dead."

"Capone, your mother ever teach you to cook?"

"A little. I know my way around a kitchen," Al responds.

"Bolognaise for three. Join us after you finish," I say.

I pick up a third chair and the sole bottle of chianti off the floor that hadn't been shot up or smashed. Thirty minutes later, the three of us laughed, drank, and ate spaghetti. Just three fucking gangsters enjoying a meal from the old country with 16 or 17 dead bodies around us. This is how it should be. You win a gunfight like this, you feast over the dead. They weren't good enough to win, so who gives a shit. Pass the fucking breadsticks.

Chapter 7
CALLING MY SHOT

New York City, New York – November 1928

The next eight years were a fucking blur for me. With the booze flowing and money rolling harder than a recently out of the closet gay man at ULTRA, I felt untouchable. I knew everyone in the city, the richest of the rich, and they were all investing with me and my firm. The parties had become so legendary, that if you weren't there, you were deemed a fucking loser. Some people even showed up with cash at the door to invest just get into the parties, which I was cool with. Money is money, holmes. As long as my palms stayed greener than *Godzilla's* dick, you could do whatever the fuck you wanted at my soirée.

The stock market was rolling and daddy was all in at every last turn. I had moved every dollar in my bank account into the Dow. I didn't just want to be rich, I wanted to rule the fucking world. Capone ended up getting promoted and is basically running the city of Chicago now, which housed the second biggest stock exchange in the U.S. We were doing a lot of deals together. When you kill people side by side with someone, you never forget it. It's a special bond you're able to laugh about forever.

In my spare time, I got to kill for Joe the Boss, which satisfied my violent murder fantasies. I needed that release. During this time, he started quarrelling with another mob boss named Salvatore Maranzano. He'd send me out on the occasional onesie/twosie hits here and there, just because I enjoyed killing motherfuckers—which he found hilarious. I did it for free too. Some things never really leave your system.

As cool as the mob ties were, no one *really* wants to party with the actual mob however. It would be too intense and people wouldn't be able to let loose. Lucky for me, these guys didn't really party like me and my friends anyway. Truthfully, the higher level guys didn't throw down like that. They were more into discreet prostitutes and bullshit like that. Look, I love prosties, I just don't want to be discreet about it.

In real life, the mob didn't want people acting all wild and shit around them, and to me, most of their traditions from "the old country" were fucking boring. I was the guy everyone wanted to hang brains with on the weekend, not those assholes. It also helped that I didn't owe them anything. I paid for my liquor like a goddamn man, in cash none the less, and I never really asked for anything more... except when I needed like two pounds of coke here and there. Again, I paid cash, so fuck you.

Some of the lower level guys would roll through to blow off some steam, and I kept a couple of them at the door to make sure no one caused any real trouble. Besides for the occasional lawyer getting riled up because he caught me porking his lady, no one really raised hands at my events. They were too high end, so shit didn't pop off like that. We were just starting to enter the age of celebrity and fame press wise. The people who stopped by wanted to be seen, and the papers usually kept a photographer on my block so they could snap some shots. You might say this was the birth of paparazzi.

I didn't mind it, because it only helped bring in a higher caliber of people, which allowed me to get more business for my firm. There was only one celebrity I couldn't stand in New York City at the time, but I didn't have a choice but to put up with his bullshit because everyone wanted to meet him. It was that cocksucker Babe Ruth from the New York Yankees. Jesus Christ that guy never shut the fuck up. He thought he owned the city, which in fairness, he probably did at the time… *except at my house.* Every time he got lippy, I didn't let him forget who the fuck I was.

One night, a doctor introduced me to this actress, Gertrude Astor was her name. A pouty blonde who was all legs and a set of tits. If memory serves me, she was 5'11" pushing six, which I never shy away from. Sometimes you gotta climb the giraffe to eat leaves from the heavens. Sorry. That's just a fancy euphemism for eating pussy. It started off strong and I'm sure I originally meant it to be poetic in my mind, but the drugs are really creeping in on me. You get it.

Anywho, I never knew who any of these actresses were, because I worked for a living and I didn't have time to see movies or any of that bullshit. Guo did, because he's Asian and they worship American pop culture, so he would usually make the intro and whisper in my ear what flicks they had been in and I'd fake a conversation like I gave a shit. Classic Saint James.

As Guo winks and walks away, I hand her a martini. "So, I hear you're an actress? What is your latest film?"

"*Shanghied*," she says flirtatiously.

"Did you go yellow face for that one? Is that why Guo seems so pissed off?"

"Um, no."

"Are you sure? I've been over there and I've never seen any honkies like you out in those rice patties. A tall drink like yourself probably required a shit ton of yellow to cover this whole surface," I say as I point up and down the entire length of her body.

She laughs. "The title of the movie was a play on words."

"Oh yeah? How many words did you have in that film?"

"I didn't have any," she says as she takes anther drink.

"WHAT THE FUCK? ARE YOU A FUCKING EXTRA? GUO, GET THE EXTRA OUT OF MY HOUSE. I DEFINITELY DON'T PUT UP WITH ANY OF THAT BULLSHIT UP IN HERE!"

The party completely stops as Guo looks at me, waving his hand under his neck for me to cut it off. Gertrude leans in and squeezes my arm, before whispering—

"The films are silent. No one has any dialogue in films right now."

"Really? Then what would you say you do in them?"

"Well, I *act* like whatever character I'm being told to play."

"Weird man. I'll fucking continue the charade. Who were you told to *act* like in Shanghied?"

"A whore."

"You don't say? How does one prepare for that role?"

"Well, I fucked a lot of dudes," she says as we share a laugh.

I can't tell if she's being serious, but I admire her moxie. She downs her cocktail in one fail swoop and sucks the olive off the toothpick. You can tell she's somewhat sophisticated, but definitely wants a man with power. Plus, after pounding that drink, it doesn't make a dent. She's used to the night life and I can tell this is going to be a real goddamn good time.

After a few more, we make our way upstairs to a private bar where I would keep a handful of the hottest women for the whales who were coming in. The ones who needed a little convincing on "closing the deal." Wink. These were the most sophisticated prostitutes in the city and we had a great deal worked out. The women never got too fucked up, did whatever weird shit my clients asked for sexually, with or without clown makeup. Most of these guys just wanted to have a casual night out of cheating on their spouse, then go home to their wife and kids. Their wives were respectable women, but you definitely couldn't choke or spit on them. That's why prosties are the best. You pay anyone enough money and you can piss on their grandparents after sex. Dead or alive. Your choice.

The upstairs bar also served as a nice reprieve for me when I wanted to take the night down a notch. It was an environment where everyone felt comfortable… until Babe fucking Ruth rolled in. This fucking guy was a wrecking ball, he'd get shit-tard hammered drunk, tell everyone how great he was, then demand to get his dick sucked in front of everyone while standing on top of a piano stool. No lie, he'd make everyone watch. *Literally everyone.* Well, on this night, I'd had enough of this fat fuck. It was time to show him who the real "King Of New York" was, the guy in a pinstripe suit, not the pinstripe uniform.

"Bartender, give me a bottle of scotch!" Babe yelled out, slightly out of breath from the walk up the stairs.

The entire room stops and laughs at him as if they were appeasing a grizzly after their child had snuck into the bear cage. He was a fat, sweaty mess in a wife beater who at some point in the night, lost his sport coat and tie. Truthfully, Babe Ruth was just another drunk asshole us rich people put up with as to not fuck up the "momentum" of the city. Manhattan was winning and so were the Yanks. Normally, I let it be… until he took one of his fat goddamn sausage fingers and tapped his cigar, ashing it onto my imported Himalayan pure yak carpet.

The bartender, an Italian man in his 40's looks over at me and shrugs. "What do you want me to do Saint James?"

"Give him one," I reply. "And give him an ashtray too."

"Why the fuck are you asking him?" Ruth gristles at the bartender.

"Because you're in the house that Street James built now and I'm Saint James Street James."

"And I just won the fucking World Series!"

"Which I could have bought the outcome of, so let's not pretend you did it on your own. You play a child's game for a living at a yearly salary I make in just under an hour every single day on Wall Street. Enjoy your drink, smoke your Cuban mud shovel, and shut the fuck up. If I wanted to hear a fat man scream all night, I'd lock you inside a pie factory cuffed to two greased wild boars."

"You may be richer than me, but I'm a goddamn hero. No one will even remember your name when you die."

"You want me to get him out of here, Street?" The bartender asks as the tense crowd looks on.

"No, we're fine. Fat man uses stick to hit even *fatter* ball and calls himself a hero? What a fucking joke. How big is that ball fat man?"

"What?"

"Look, I know you're dumb as shit, because your parents only put four letters in your first and last name so you'd be able to spell it—but you must at least know the size of the fucking baseball you hit every day for a living. What's the circumference?"

He's starting to get *really* pissed. "Nine and a quarter inches."

"Great. Now here's *another* nine and a quarter inches," I say as I yank my pants to the floor. I take both hands and wrap them around my cock, swinging it like I'm in the batter's box waiting for a pitch.

"Hey man, put your dick away. Nobody wants to see that," he says trying to muster up some bravery. I can tell he's clearly uncomfortable now.

"On the contrary, everyone wants to see it. They've seen it since I was a boy. Thousands of people used to line up at the state fair paying a nickel a piece just to get a glimpse of it. And if they were real lucky, on the right night, I'd tie fishing line around it, stick a couple of bottle caps on my balls, and put it on a charcuterie board—just to make it tap dance for them while my father accompanied me with an accordion."

This is a big boy flex and he knows it. When a man isn't afraid to pull his dick out at a high class party in front of a World Series Champion, chances are—whatever is about to happen—ain't going to be good for the other man calling him out. Time to hit the gas and blow right through the red light. I pick up the speed in my "swing."

"I think we're all good here, pal. I'm going to head downstairs now—

"Not a fucking prayer, *Babe*. Tonight we're going to show these fine people what *real* skill is. You—how long does it take for this fat fuck to round the bases after a home run?" I ask as I point to nebbish banker in his 50's named Bob Hemphill.

"I don't know, a minute I'd say," he says as he takes a sip of his martini. Now everyone's curiosity is peaked.

"That sounds generous to me, Bob. To make this more interesting, let's say you're right. One minute for this barrel to roll over Niagara. I'll bet you I can make this girl, who I just met, cum in under a minute and call my shot in the process."

"Call your shot? What does that mean?" Babe asks.

I squeeze my now hard dick with one hand and point it toward an empty shot glass resting on the bar, which is about ten feet away. The small gathering begins to laugh as I wink at the shot glass. An older woman faints and falls down the entire length of the staircase. No one else bothers to assist, that's how bad they want to see this. (She died peacefully in the hospital several days later surrounded by loved ones.) The Babe is now backed into a corner. He has to bet *and* watch me fuck.

"You're going to blow a load in that shot glass?"

"Every last drop. If I miss, you win. Pretty fucking simple, right?"

"I'll take that bet," he says with a smirk.

"Swell. How much do you make a season?"

"$70,000."

"That's it? Well, let's bet that."

Babe folds his arms nervously and stammers, "You must be joking?"

"My dick is still hard, so obviously I'm not joking. Bartender, please show the *hero* that I'm not joking."

The bartender reaches under the bar and pulls out a suitcase with a hundred grand in it and pops it open. He removes 70K in cash and stacks it neatly next to the shot glass. Everyone nods their heads impressed.

"Bob, you got an eye on that watch?"

Bob holds up his wrist with a gold watch and smiles. "On my count Saint James, okay?"

Gertrude pulls her panties down, bends over, and hikes her skirt up above her waist— assuming your classic doggy style posish. I tap her ass like it's home plate, before spitting into my hands and "re-gripping" my dick like Moises Alou. She looks back and smiles.

"You make me cum in under a minute, I might have to marry you," she says seductively.

"Gertrude, you should be so lucky," I whisper.

Bob looks at his watch and points to me with his finger, "And go!"

I quickly insert Gertrude from behind and grab her hips at ten and two faster than an Asian in driving school their first time behind the wheel. *This wasn't my first time obviously.* My stroke game was tighter than Clarence Carter, and right around the forty-eight second mark I could see her knees buckle like a prize fighter who had taken too much punishment in the "Championship Rounds." Home girl begins to scream like Jody Foster in *Nell*.

"Tay in da wind, tay in da wind," she yells, gyrating her arms before using them to break her fall as she hit the ground in ecstasy.

I give three quick jerks to mah dong with my right hand, like I'm pumping a shotgun, as I unleash a triple roper that floats through the air like a butterfly on mescaline before landing perfectly inside the shot glass. Daddy didn't miss one single drop. It was a fucking walk off. The small crowd erupts in cheers as they eagerly look over at Bob.

"59 seconds flat!" Bob exclaims holding up his watch proudly.

I quickly pull up my pants and hold my index finger toward the sky, hoping all of my dead relatives saw what I just did tonight. Babe shakes his head in disbelief. I pull out a heater from my pocket and light it, then put my dick hand on his shoulder. He needed to feel the warmth of that palm.

"I'll send a man to pick up your salary in the morning. You fucking work for me now next year, big shit. If I want tickets for my clients, you will accommodate me with the best seats in the house. And motherfucker every time I'm there, you better give a wink and a tip of the cap to whomever I'm with. Game recognizes game, so every time you see me, I want you to acknowledge the best to ever do it. You understand me, bleu cheese?"

He nods despondently as I begin to walk away. "I just got one question. How did you do it?" Babe asks in wonderment.

I turn back to him and smile. "I'm the greatest cocksman who ever lived. You want to be a real hero, call your shot one day."

Bob taps me on the shoulder. "Uh, Saint James? I'm not sure sexually what is happening with the girl, but she appears to be having a full blown epileptic seizure."

I look over as Gertrude violently shakes on the floor, curled up in the fetal position. "That's normal. She should be alert and aware of her surroundings in about 45 seconds. Put two fingers in her mouth so she doesn't swallow her tongue."

"Okay," Bob says kind of freaked out.

"When she comes to, let her know that she'll probably have epilepsy for life. Tell her to avoid sunlight and other huge penises. It will only trigger her new condition. I gotta go," I say as I glide down the stairs like Fred Astaire on pure MDMA.

The bartender puts away the money in the briefcase, downs my shot of jizz, and jumps out the window committing suicide. I understand it. He'll never see anything like that the rest of his life and he was ready to end it. Most people have a hard time reconciling that the rest of their lives are meaningless after witnessing something like that. He didn't and I applaud him for his honesty.

The twenty or so party goers who got to witness it first hand told that story that rest of their lives. I heard years later that Babe Ruth himself called his own shot in the World Series, and imitation is the sincerest form of crab meat. I wasn't around to see it because baseball is fucking boring. All

I know is that he never showed up at one of my parties again… but the Feds did that night.

As soon as I hit the bottom stairs, I was served with a fucking warrant. A smarmy motherfucker in his 40's named Ernest Conroy, a real ballbuster, slapped it against my chest. I briefly give it a looksee before wiping my cock off with it and handing it back to him. It was still wet and you could smell the pussy on it.

"You're under arrest for not following the Prohibition Act," Ernest says.

"The Prohibition Act is bullshit and America needs to drink or we'd all be fucking hardos like you having missionary sex once a month. Daddy likes to get his beak wet and sexually explore like Lewis and Clark."

Conroy looks at me confused. "Lewis and Clark? I'm not tracking?"

"Why do you think Lewis named his dog Seamen, because he was a proficient sailor? Everyone knows they each took turns fucking that dog on long trips—

"You're really drunk, sir. We're taking you into the station. Everybody clear out! The party is over!"

Gertrude is still screaming from upstairs as the guests start to walk down the enormous staircase. Babe Ruth stumbles down and the other Feds begin to elbow each other with enormous smiles. One of the younger Feds walks over to Conroy and whispers in his ear.

"That's the Babe!" he says excitedly.

Conroy nods, knowing who he is. He holds up his hand in front of him. "You want to explain to me what's going on here before it hits the papers tomorrow again, Babe? We got a dead body on the sidewalk."

"Well this man fucked a girl into a seizure, I lost my entire salary betting him that he couldn't nut into a shot glass half way across the room, and the bartender killed himself afterward. Just another fucking Tuesday night for the Babe. Can I go? I have a doubleheader starting a noon tomorrow and this hangover is going to be rectal."

"Sure thing, Champ. Saint James, you come with us. I want to know who your supplier is," Conroy says as he cuffs me and leads me out.

"Guo, call my lawyer. Have him meet me at the station. Tell him to bring some coke or I'm not going to be worth a shit to anyone in the morning."

"You got it, boss."

The rest of the party left peacefully. At that moment, I figured the point of it all was to bust me in front of my high powered friends and embarrass me. It turned out to be much deeper than that. They wanted to see old Saint James Street James behind bars, not only because I was breaking the law underneath their nose, but because they hated the man I worked with and wanted to bring down the whole operation. Girls just want to fun, but sometimes other people don't want them to. Quoting Cindy Lauper is a shitty way to end a chapter for you aspiring writers out there. I still take the time out to teach. You're welcome.

Chapter 8

A BIRD IN THE HAND IS WORTH TWO IN HER BUSH

New Year's Eve 1928

Obviously, New Year's Eve at the Street James household was an all out fucking rager. I'm not a big holiday guy, but I enjoy New Year's Eve and of course, Thanksgiving. Celebrating the white man taking over an entire country by goading the Indians in with turkey and gravy has always made me laugh. Still does to this day. New Year's Eve was more sentimental, however. I took immense joy in looking back at the last twelve months and the success I had, then at the stroke of midnight getting my dick sucked by three strange women while drinking champagne.

This New Year's was different though, probably because I was experimenting with multiple drugs at the same time, which is commonly known as "candy flipping." After squeezing off my second load into some girl's mouth, I lower myself down from the chandelier and begin to take the bear trap off my leg. As I remove it, a beautiful designer named Marla walks over with a glass of champagne for me.

"We have a half hour before midnight, you want to walk down to Times Square with me and see the ball drop?"

"Why the fuck would I want to do that stupid shit?"

"It's your ball?"

"What?"

"I made a cast out of your right testicle last month and used it as my inspiration to design the new ball dropping in Times Square. Don't you remember?" She asks puzzled.

"To be real, people are plastering up my sack and dong twice a month. One chick wanted used my plaster shaft to build a drinking well for children over in Namibia. This other trick hung my plaster cock above her husband's night stand as some sort of vision board or something to look up to— what I'm saying is, I can't keep track. If my ball is going to bring in the New Year, then yeah, I'm down to see that."

"Great, let me grab my jacket and scarf," she says before making her way to the coat room down the hall.

When I pull my pants up, I notice the drugs are really starting to take hold of me. I was rocked and definitely in no condition to walk the streets with a million other grimy motherfuckers who were too poor to throw a real party. Seriously, the shit is dirty down there. They pack these Chinamen in there starting at like 6am. They're all diapered up so they can save their spot closest to the ball by avoiding bathroom breaks. God knows how many times they've pissed themselves throughout the course of the day waiting for that thing to drop. This is the first and last time I would be doing it. EVER. Let me explain.

As Marla and I walk arm in arm down 6th street toward the chaos, I start hallucinating on a level that I had never been to before. I know it seems like I say that a lot, but just know that every single time I do, it really is the most fucked up I've ever been. I'm not sorry that I keep surpassing myself.

For instance, right now my goal is to get up close to see my ball drop, so I punch a cop in the face who is casually walking by and drag him into an ally to strip him down. I then proceed to put on his uniform and escort Marla through the crowd. Anyone who gets in my way, I take out my night stick and violently let them know how weak the back of their knees are. Being in uniform and hopped up on this many drugs gave me an enormous sense of power. Marla squeezes my bicep like a stroke victim. I grab her wrist and examine it.

"Are you wearing a medical bracelet and is there something I need to inject into you? Fucking blink for me!"

"There's nothing wrong. I've just always wanted to have sex with a man in uniform," she says.

"Cool let's do that. Let's bang that mailman over there," I say, pointing out an elderly mailman in his mid 60's holding hands with his wife. "I'll let you take her out with the nightstick if you want so you can experience the feeling?"

She stares at me strangely. "No, I want to have sex with *you*. You're wearing a uniform."

"Oh. Sorry about that. I am so high right now that I forgot that actually happened. Time is a flat circle and the earth moves with—

"Just shut the fuck up and kiss me. There's thirty seconds until midnight," she says as she grabs my face and starts making out with me.

Here's where things get tricky and why "sometimes" copious amounts of drugs aren't always the best thing. As the crowd begins to count down from twenty, I start to lose my balance. Marla and I fall back through the crowd—past the actual police in front of the ball itself as it begins to drop. I'm not sure if they thought I was one of them and that's why nobody stopped us, or maybe they were amped to see one of their boys getting ass on New Year's? Who fucking knows? What I can tell you is that we were making out so hard, that once we were through the crowd of people, my momentum took us right to the ground. Marla sits on top of me laughing. She looked so stunning underneath the New York City lights.

"You want to get married?" I ask.

"What? You barely know me? I'm just some dumb girl who made a plaster cast of your testicle," she says, slightly blushing.

"I know, but it's New Year's Eve. It's a time for new beginnings."

"Are you being serious?"

"Yes. Let's just fucking do it."

The crowd grows louder and louder chanting, "5, 4, 3—

"Ye—*aaaaaaaaaafuuuuuuuuck*—

In that instant, the ball drops, crushing her head backward and completely breaking her neck and back in half.

She folds up like an accordion on top of me. Luckily, that goddamn thing stopped about 2 and half feet from the ground. Six more inches and I would have died myself. Remember when I said she looked "so stunning underneath the New York City lights?"

Well, it turns out that those "lights" were attached to the ball itself and we were on the ground underneath it. The good news is that ball broke her neck immediately and she died instantly. Why does this keep happening to me? Whatever. It was horrific and it turned out to be a major precursor of things to come as 1929 came in like a wrecking ball. Turns out it was my own ball. Who knew?

After twenty-five minutes I was finally able to extricate myself from her body and the New Year's Ball itself. Surprisingly, no one really notices because everyone is caught up in the moment. I wish I could have seen the look on whoever the poor fucker's face that found Marla the next morning. I'm sure they had a lot of questions. Not. My. Problem.

What is my problem, is the tremendous amount of blood all over me. Thank fuck for the cop uniform, which provided every excuse I need. The entire walk home men tip their caps toward me as they shield their women. There was so much blood that no one had the heart to even ask what had happened, and obviously I play along and tip my cap back, not wanting to break character. I made it all the way to my front door, before someone actually said one word to me. It was my 80-year-old bitch ass neighbor Agnes, who was poking her head out of the window instead of just dying at her age like everyone else did in the 1920's. She was fucking mortified.

"Oh dear God! What happened?" Agnes said clutching her pearls exactly like a white woman does in a sitch like this.

"Well Agnes, let's just say the sea turtle exhibit at the zoo will be closed for awhile and leave it at that, okay? I did what I could. Have a good night and Happy Fucking New Year's."

I walk in and slam the door, completely forgetting that I had thrown a massive New Year's Eve party and everyone was still here. Fucking *drugas*. Shockingly, no one said anything to me. If you're going to accidently kill someone, do it on New Year's Eve in a cop uniform in New York City. No one says shit to you. Obviously, I wasn't in the mood to party anymore so I pop a couple downers, take off my clothes next to the bed, and tuck myself in and go to sleep. Seconds later, I felt a familiar hand on my cock. It was the weird girl from eight years ago. I'm assuming she had a rough night as well, so I just let it go. It felt nice having a woman with a pulse on my cock again.

The following morning, I was awoken by Guo, who handed me a message on a piece of paper. I knew it had to be important, because no wakes me up before 2pm otherwise. When I open up the note, it reads: "**Coffee Shop. High noon. Come alone. Joe.**" Guo then hands me a mirror with five lines of that "Columbian Retirement Package" to pile drive down just so I could get out of bed.

My feet hit the floor like I stepped out of the front door of 875 South Bundy Drive the night a certain someone went to Chicago. There was blood everywhere and enough evidence to convict me without a pair of Isotoners. I look down at the bloody clothes beneath my feet, then shrug at Guo.

"What if I told you it was an accident?"

"Does it matter to you?" Guo asks.

"That question is super deep and I'd be stoked to answer that literally any other time than right now, but you know how hungover I am, so instead just shut the fuck up and burn my clothes while I go wash off my ding dong."

"The best time to plant a tree was twenty years ago. The second best time is today," he says as he picks up my bloody clothes.

"Talk does not cook rice, Guo. We can trade ancient Chinese proverbs all goddamn day if we want to. It still isn't going to bring back that girl who died on my cock last night as a three ton replica of my right nut crushed her in half on top of me."

I throw a bird up behind my back as I walk to my all white marble shower, which was completely renovated after the 1920 Olympics nine years ago. Deep red blood swirls down the drain and I was reminded of how much death has followed me over the last decade. Then I wonder why the coke hadn't made a dent yet. I was in rough shape. Deep down, I wish I could have gone back to bed, but I didn't have a choice. Joe rarely asked for meetings like this one on one, so

I knew it had to be important. In hindsight, I should have skipped the meeting and chalked it up to New Year's Eve shenannies, but instead I coughed and felt my proud two strain—letting my testicular fortitude get the best of me. This meeting would ultimately alter the course of my life.

After I manage to pull myself together, I grab my hat from Guo who was holding it by the door, and we head down to the coffee shop. It wasn't far, maybe a couple blocks, but the cold air made it feel like I was trekking through the Adirondacks. I haven't felt a chill in the air like this since my Civil War days and I remember thinking to myself how odd it was that I had essentially forgot about that period of my life in the 1860's. It seems like a lifetime ago, which to most people my age, it is.

When I step inside, I spot Joe the Boss sipping coffee at a table by himself in the middle of café. Joe was a lot like Stonewall Jackson, they were both equally stubborn and steadfast in their beliefs, and those beliefs were fucking ridiculous. Eventually they would die on that hill for something they could never control anyway. Times change, but assholes don't.

I take my coat and gloves off, handing them to Guo who stands by the door, before walking over to greet Joe. He shakes my hand and extends a chair for me to sit in across from him with my back toward the window, which I still hate to this day. Never sit with your back toward the window, no matter what. I pour myself a cup of coffee as I look over my shoulder at Guo.

"How was your New Year's Eve, Saint James?" Joe asks.

"Usual. Boy meets girl. Girl makes a testicle replica of boy. Girl gets crushed to death by replica. That story is as old as time."

He stares at me in disbelief. "You're a weird fucking guy."

"I am? Come on. I'm not the one drinking coffee in an empty café on New Year's Day ominous as shit. Where the fuck are your bodyguards anyway?"

"I never need a bodyguard when you're around. I know you're strapped to the teeth and I can trust you," he says pointing at my shoulder holsters.

"Yeah, but still, aren't you in a war with the Casternellas? I've heard whispers at my parties. And not the type of whispers that you hear when you smoke too much weed and think you hear voices in the forest while you search for a missing kite."

"That's why I'm here. The rumors you hear are true, which is why I asked you to come today. I'd like you to take on a bigger role in my family business. Be my trigger man, so to speak. I can't trust anyone these days but you. You've never changed in the ten years since I've known you."

"Truthfully, I haven't changed in a hundred plus, but that's another story for a different day. I appreciate the offer, but I must respectfully decline. My life is great. I get my dick sucked on the reg. The stock market is rolling and I genuinely feel like I might live forever at this point."

"No one lives forever, Saint James. No one really wants to deep down. Eventually we all get to an age where we become careless and it ends. Either by your choice, or someone else's."

I nod as we sit in silence, thinking for a moment as we drink our coffee. All these years later he was right. Today, sitting here writing my memoirs as we speak, I didn't really put the proper value on the word "careless" when he said it. Being careless can go one of two ways, you can be reckless with your actions and become careless, or you could stop caring about the world around you which in turn makes you care *less*. The latter is exactly where I'm at in 2015.

"How bad is it going to get? Can this be talked out over a meal?" I ask as I set my coffee down.

"I'm not sure I want to. This fucking guy Casternella, he's a poor cunt from the shittiest part of the old country. He's a fucking peasant to me. All of those people are. I don't have anything in common with him."

"Give me his address, let me talk to him. This isn't anything that can't be solved with four or five bottles of gin and an orgy—

Before I could finish my sentence, three men burst through the front door of the coffee shop with guns blazing. The first man takes out Guo, turning his head into a canoe as he tries to draw his weapon. Before I could even pull my pistols from my shoulder holster, four of Joe's bodyguards appear from the kitchen and begin mowing down the men with Tommy guns. Joe runs out of the back as the men move in closer. The only man that remains was the man that wet down Guo. I wave off Joe's guys, letting them know that I want that kill.

The smarmy fuck who did this was fresh out of bullets, and here we stand toe to toe. With both pistols now removed from my holsters, I begin to fire with both hands at the same time. He doesn't have much time left on this earth, but I want him to feel every last second of it. The first two shots I fire go right into his shoulders. Then, I carefully move down to his hands, firing two bullets into each meat hook. After that, I blast holes in each of his knees, and then his ankles. Those are ones you don't think about, but they cause unbearable pain when pierced by bullets.

As this Wop fuck lies on the ground screaming and writhing in pain, I shoot him right through the abdomen. Despite all of these wounds, he was still alive. I slowly walk over to him and stand over his body as I see my dead friend slumped over in the background. This fucker holds his hands up, covered in blood.

"Please don't kill me. I got a family at home. I want to live," he begs.

"Newsflash hombre, you ain't going to live. And that man you killed *was* my only family, so I'm all done with this bullshit. You've been shot eight times and you got about two minutes left before you bleed out. Who do you work for?"

"Fuck you!" he screams as he spits a huge, thick wad of blood at me, which hits my lower pant leg.

"What is the hope and dream behind spitting on me? Why do people do that when they're dying? I don't give a shit about your last second attempt at faking dignity, and it makes me even more angrier that I have to get this dry cleaned. Now you lose a couple fingers, motherfucker."

I blast off the middle fingers off each his hands. Part of me even thought about re-circing this guy just so whoever finds him would appreciate my handy work. Before you type "recirc" into your Google machine, it means "re-circumcising." You're welcome. His writhing on the floor continues as boredom is starting to kick in for me.

"Awww fuck! Jesus! Why don't you just end this?" He asks, waving his bloody hands around, which only contain eight digits now.

"I'll take those index fingers off next and leave you with two lobster claws if you don't tell me who you work for. You'll be dead momentarily anyway, so what the fuck do you care?" I ask as I raise my pistols.

He flinches and coughs up more blood. "Fine. Fuck you. The Casternellas! Look, don't take this as a personal thing against you or anything, we were just here to kill *him*. Please! You gotta believe me!"

"You don't storm a coffee shop with four men firing machine guns to stop in for an expresso, you didn't give a shit who was in here. We all had to go. Am I right?"

I raise my both guns at his forehead prepared to end his existence, when all of the sudden I hear the bells ring from above the top of the front door. There's a shadowy figure holding something underneath a towel or maybe some type of curtain. It's hard to tell. The arm of the figure raises and the curtain extends. It now appears to be some type of gun and I can't take the risk. I raise up and someone screams—

"HE'S GOT A GUN! HE'S GOT A FUCKING GUN!"

It's difficult to see where the voice is coming from before the towel lifts up completely, so I fire one shot toward the figure. I hear a loud internal, guttural sound, then an object hits the floor. As I move toward the thud on the ground, I see that it's a rare African parrot. The person that was holding it, whips off the bulky winter jacket she was wearing and begins crying. It's a cute thirty-something librarian who's now hovering over the animal, standing there completely devastated. I fire one shot into the dude's head I was already about to kill, so I could give my full attention to the poor woman and her bird. Tears stream down her face.

"Why would you even do that?" She asked, extremely hurt.

"That guy was going to die anyway. It was more of a case of how fast versus—

"No! Why would you kill my parrot?"

"Why the fuck does a woman of your age carry a parrot around town? I'm willing to wager you're probably still not married?"

"My work with birds is more important than any relationship with a man!" she fires back.

"I understand that sentiment, but I think I could change your mind. I have the craziest murder boner right now and you may never have another opportunity like this in your entire life to bone a guy who just committed multiple homicides. It's a life changer. Guaranteed four orgasms at a minimum. I promise."

"Are you trying to have sex with me right now after all that just happened? Look around you."

The second this sentence escapes her mouth, NYPD busts through the doors throwing me to the ground. As I'm cuffed on the floor, I'm face to face with the almost lifeless parrot, whose breathing is labored. He looks me dead in the eye and squawks—

"What did the pirate do after the parrot bit off his dick?"

"I don't know, what?"

"He got a woodpecker," the parrot says before closing his eyes.

This completely enrages me. I hate shitty jokes more than anything in this world, so I lunge at the parrot trying to head-butt it to death. The police pick me up off the floor as I struggle, now trying to kick the bird. That motherfucker. As they're pulling me out of the front door of the coffee shop, I turn my head back toward the woman.

"I'm still down for that sex by the way. The whole handcuff thing is only enhancing my whole sitch that I told you about a minute ago."

She shakes her head and puts her coat over her dead bird as they place me into the back of a cop car. On the ride over to the jail, my mind was mostly absent. I was still hungover from the night before, which made the gunfight and the death of Guo seem distant. The only thing I could think about that was that shitty joke the parrot told me before closing his eyes the entire way there. Fuck that thing.

Chapter 9
MURDER WAS THE CASE THAT THEY GAVE ME

October 21, 1929

For eight months leading up to my trial, I sat in the Manhattan Detention Complex known as "The Tombs", because it was allegedly modeled after an ancient Egyptian tomb. How fucking clever. It was some low level shit where no one really bothered you if you paid off the guards. You could definitely have as many conjugals as you want, so obviously, I was fucking daily up in that bitch. Sometimes I would sit and reset for twenty, then go another round just out of boredom. That's the real motherfucker about jail; it's boring as shit.

The girls were stuffing drugs in their prison wallet so we avoided anal, that way I could get my fix. Having money in jail solves most of the day to day mundaneness of it all. I could get through almost anything with women and drugs, so I rode it out until the trial just fine. This was temporary after all. The DA didn't really have shit in this case, so I was biding my time until the trial ended.

The librarian woman who walked in with the fucking parrot was basically the only witness… *and she ended up dead in a river about four months ago.* This really upset me, mostly because I never got to bone her. What a waste of a perfectly good murder boner. I know I shouldn't dwell on it, but I always think about the women I didn't get to insert in this life. It's my cross to bear, I guess. Jesus had one, so why shouldn't I?

Each and every girl I never got to "beat them guts in" I can see so vividly in my mind to this very day. I can't remember what color my shit was this afternoon, but I can tell you that librarian looking chick had great cheek bones, unusually high arched feet, and a modest C-cup that had room for more growing with a couple kids. RIP Linda, or whatever the fuck your name is. What? I never said I was good at names.

Joe The Boss had her iced as my case got closer to trial after he made sure I wasn't going to snitch. Since I had his trust, this allowed me the classic "self defense" tale. Other than your usual set of "innocent bystanders" who gave vague descriptions of screaming and gunshots, the prosecution had nothing. Just one rich white man's word against a bunch of strangers who were across the street, too bundled up to see shit on a cold January day.

The media and photographers were out in full force once the trial got started. My side of the courtroom was filled with harlots, including the chick who always grabbed my cock off and on for nine years, which I appreciated. The elitists I use to hang with on a nightly basis now wanted nothing to do with me. I expected that.

Look, people go where the money and parties are. Once that ends, they move on to the next soirée. There's no hard feelings and nothing to get butt hurt about. The show goes on with or without you, and right now, there hasn't been a party for nine months in my world. I wouldn't want to sit at some goddamn boring trial either. Matter of fact, it'd be rad to be doing coke with them right now. The people in documentaries that are always "shocked they had no one to turn to" are fucking losers. Grow up. You went to jail, they didn't. End of story. Let them live their lives.

The courtroom erupted as I was led in wearing a suit that Gianni Versace would have punched his gay lover to death for, before taking his own life in it. I'm sure he would have rather gone out this way than getting his head blown off, I can promise you that. The judge was old as shit, but I still caught a peek of him slipping his hand under his robe, obviously impressed by my whole shit. We had this in the bag. My lawyer, Slim Danny, rolled in moments later completely sandwich-less. I couldn't help but chuckle as he sat down.

"No sammy today, Danny?" I asked sarcastically.

"Not unless you want this trial to last two years, and I don't know if you can afford that my friend," he said as he opened his briefcase and began to shuffle some papers on the desk.

"Of course I can. Why wouldn't I be able to? I'm rich as fuck."

"Have you been reading the papers? I hope you've diversified your funds. The market isn't doing so hot."

I was a little taken back by this statement. "No, I don't read the paper in the goddamn pokey. Matter of fact, I usually line the floor with it during Conjugals as some kind of a catch pad. The guards aren't cool with me blasting loads all over the joint."

"Well, I'd take a day off and give the Times a quick glance. If the market crashes, it's all over. You'll end up working for Joe full time and you see where that gets you," he says motioning to the court room circus behind us.

"I've never worked *for* him in the first place. I worked *with* him. There's a big difference my man."

"You sure about that? I don't see him sitting here or the four people that magically popped out of the kitchen. Look, you got nothing to worry about in this one. No witnesses, no big deal. This should wrap up in a week or so. Afterward, I would reevaluate your acquaintances and diversify your assets. You can never be too careful. Trust me, I've been doing this a long time, and I've seen many men crossed up by their own arrogance."

I leap on top of the table and raise my arms toward the sky, whipping the crowd into a frenzy. The judge bangs his gavel as I stomp my feet a la Michael Jackson on top of that limo after he was acquitted. I take it all in and smile at Slim Danny before I take my seat.

"You just fucking worry about your job. I'll be fine."

"Okay. Don't say I didn't warn you, Saint James. Let me ask you one last question before we start?"

"What's that Slim?"

Danny leans in real close to me and gets a few inches from my face before saying, "Can you smell any pussy on my moustache?"

"You dirty motherfucker! You know I can brother!"

Slim Danny fist bumps me as the judge begins the proceedings. He then slips me a baggie of Chuck Sheen, which I immediately double nostril under the desk to properly entertain myself from this nonsense. I couldn't tell you who the first witness was, I was so blasted on coke. Honestly, it didn't really matter, none of Joe's people ratted on me and it was pretty much a snooze fest. One by one, gimp ass street witnesses came to the stand and basically said the same thing over and over in a slightly different variation—

"I heard loud gunshots."

"It sounded like chaos in there."

"There was blood on the windows."

"His penis seemed completely erect when the cops led him out in handcuffs."

"It seemed like a baby's arm trying to punch through a garbage bag."

"I couldn't tell where the man began and the penis ended."

You get it. After a week of this haberdashery, I was ready for this to be done with. I obviously flashed my dong a few times to the jury throughout the testimony, and threw a few winks toward the lady jurors just so they knew it *could* have been true. It was a fun, flirty, trial all the way up till the end. I didn't have a care in the world... until the prosecution approached the bench to hand the judge a slip of paper with the last witness on it. I could tell I was in trouble by the look in his eyes. He pulls his glasses off his face after reading it and stares at the prosecution incredulously.

"Who is Carl Caruthers?"

"He's the only person who was in the room at the time of the murders, your honor," the prosecutor replies.

The entire courtroom gasps. Slim Danny furiously digs through his briefcase trying to find out who "Carl Caruthers" is. I eye-fuck the shit out of him, thinking he turned on me, or at the very least—Joe The Boss did. He shrugs his shoulders and stands up, dumbfounded.

"Your honor, I object. There is no Carl Caruthers on my witness list that was turned in from the prosecution during pretrial. I am asking for this witness to be dismissed," Danny says out of breath.

"It's actually the parrot described on page four," the Judge responds.

"But that's impossible your honor, the parrot is dead—

"Now calling Carl Caruthers to the stand," he says.

The back of the courtroom doors swing open and we see a heavily bandaged parrot being escorted in a wheelchair by the bailiff. A couple of the harlots pass out on the floor as Carl is wheeled in. The parrot is basically in a full body cast, except for his head, which is exposed. Photographers start snapping off pictures left and right. Danny grabs my arm and leans into to me.

"Is that the parrot?"

"I can't see his body, but the head looks the same."

"Jesus Christ. I thought you killed him."

"So did I."

You could hear an A-cup bra drop, that's how tense the courtroom was. I put my head under the table and ingest the rest of my bag of coke, *which was supposed to last me through the end of the day*. Now that's ruined. The focus turned to how much this motherfucker would say, and more importantly, if the jury would believe him? The prosecutor smiled at me before turning to the jury.

"Ladies and gentlemen, I present to you Carl Caruthers, the infamous parrot that was shot and left presumably dead at the scene of the crime by Mr. Street James. He is the only witness who is still alive that was inside that room on New Year's Day."

Slim Danny jumps to his feet. "Your honor, I object. This is a bird who is taught vocabulary by it's owner. I'd also like to point out that his owner is dead. We don't know who taught this bird to talk. It could have been a white man who was into Jamaican music, which would make this testimony not only unbelievable, but also unbearable."

The courtroom erupts in laughter. Just as the Judge is about to bang his gavel, the parrot clears his throat. Everyone goes silent as all eyes focus on the bird, who is propped up on top of five phone books on the witness stand.

"I was there... *and I remember everything clear as day.*"

His English is perfect. Goddamnit. Slim Danny runs his fingers through his thinning hairline, then deeply inhales through his nostrils, no doubt trying to muster up a small scent of last night's pussy. I try and remain stoic, but it's hard to keep my composure. I almost wish I could have fucked his owner even more now, so he'd have something else to talk about. You have to realize; this was the first parrot to testify as a witness against someone during a trial in United States history. Below is the full testimony from the trial:

Judge: "Do you swear to tell the truth, the whole truth, and nothing but the truth, so help you God?"

Carl: "I do, your honor."

Judge: "Prosecution, you may proceed."

Prosecutor: "Thank you, your honor. Carl, you're very brave for being here today. How are you you feeling?"

Carl: "Like a set of anal beads on a nightstand in San Francisco. I can breathe, but it really stinks."

Prosecutor: "I bet. Can you describe what you saw on the afternoon of January 1st, New Year's Day, at Delfino's Coffee Shoppe?"

Carl: "It was a normal day like any other. My owner and I had come in for morning decaf lattes just like every other morning—

Slim Danny: "Objection, your honor! I'm not sure a parrot can ingest any form of coffee, let alone decaf coffee. No one drinks that in real life and the ones that do shouldn't even pretend to drink coffee at all."

Judge: "I'll allow the objection. Why were you allegedly attempting to drink decaf coffee and how is that possible for a parrot?"

Carl: "Your honor, regular coffee would run through me faster than a Kenyan four by one hundred team. Decaf is the only thing I can drink. Human cars would be destroyed permanently if that was allowed. Trust me, I've seen the aerials."

Judge: "I bet. I'll allow it. Continue the line of questioning."

Prosecutor: "Carl, where were you at 12pm on New Year's day 1929?"

Carl: "Sure. I woke up just before noon, licked my entire body clean, including my genitalia, then began my Portuguese lessons with my owner. She had met a man at a salsa class and was trying to impress him, same as any other desperate white woman in her late 30's who is unmarried with no kids. Afterward, we went to get our daily coffee. She needed a friend. A permanent one who was confined to a cage."

Prosecutor: "And when you went to the coffee shop you had gone to every day, what did you see when you walked in?"

Slim Danny: "Objection your honor! He definitely didn't walk in! We can't keep pretending to treat him like a real human."

Judge: (bangs his gavel) "He's speaking more clearly than you! I'll allow it!"

Prosecutor: "Thank you, your honor. As I was saying before, what did you see when you entered the coffee shop on the afternoon of January 1st of this year."

Carl: "My eyes first went toward a muffin of some sort, my beak was telling me blueberry initially, then I deciphered that it was definitely banana nut. That's when I noticed dead bodies strewn out across the floor. Human bodies."

Prosecutor: "Can you describe the victims?"

Carl: "They all had two arms and two legs. Same as any other humans I guess. The victims were all male."

Prosecutor: "What happened next?"

Carl: "My first instinct was to fly away. But my owner changes in front of me every day and usually throws in a masturbation sesh in front of my cage. I'm not sure if I'm her kink or whatever, but I enjoy it, and it sure beats Africa. That place is hot as fuck."

Prosecutor: "But you didn't fly away did you Carl? Instead, you stayed with your owner, and it almost cost you your life, isn't that right? You were shot moments after entering the coffee shop. Isn't that correct?"

Carl: "Yeah, I mean, I'm all fucked up in a body cast, so that's pretty obvious. Speaking of which, if you could sign it for me after this that would be pretty sweet. No one has signed my cast yet."

Prosecutor: "Of course. Can you point to the man that pulled the trigger and shot you that fateful day Carl?"

Carl: "I can't move my arms because of the cast, but I'll toss a beak his way. (The parrot points his beak at Saint James Street James and the crowd audibly gasps.)

Prosecutor: "Do you know the man you're referring to over there?"

Carl: "Yes. That's Saint James Street James. I've seen him in the news papers that line the cage I shit in. I recognize his face."

Prosecutor: "Was there anyone else with him in the coffee shop that day?"

Carl: "Not that was alive. It was just a pile of Italian dead bodies everywhere. He was the only one standing there, holding a gun."

Prosecutor: "You're positive there was no one else besides the defendant when you and your owner walked in?"

Carl: "I'm positive."

Prosecutor: "Can you remember anything else from the encounter with Saint James Street James on that afternoon?"

Carl: "Yeah, he kept asking my owner if she wanted to have sex and persisted to describe the intense murder boner he had."

Prosecutor: "I'm sorry, did you say 'murder boner'?"

Carl: "Yes."

Prosecutor: "What is a murder boner?"

Carl: "He described is as a crazy boner that a man rarely gets in this life, which is achievable only after killing a bunch of people."

Prosecutor: "Oh my. Did he elaborate any further?"

Carl: "He may have, but I went unconscious after that. The next thing I remember was waking up in a hospital four days later with my master seated in a chair in front of my bed masturbating."

Prosecutor: "Well, you're very brave for being here today. You've been extremely helpful. No further questions your honor."

Judge: "Your witness, defense."

Slim Danny: "Thank you, your honor. Mr. Caruthers, do you know what your exact vision is?"

Carl: "Worldly?"

Slim Danny: "No, I meant is it 20/20. 20/10? What is your exact vision statistically?"

Carl: "I'm sorry, I don't know what you mean?"

Slim Danny: "Have you ever been to an optometrist? And if so, what did he tell you your vision was?"

Carl: "I'm a parrot, man. I don't really get to go to an optometrist."

Slim Danny: "If you've never been to an optometrist, how do you know what your vision is?"

Prosecutor: "Objection. The defense is badgering the parrot."

Slim Danny: "Your honor, I'm trying to establish the eye sight of the bird. We're in unchartered territory at this point by allowing a wild animal on the witness stand?"

Judge: "Overruled. I'll allow it. Continue."

Slim Danny: "Thank you, your honor. Since you've never been to an optometrist, can you describe your eye sight and the average eyesight of a normal parrot? Would you say it's excellent, decent, or modest?"

Carl: "I mean, I'm not a hawk or anything, but it's alright."

Slim Danny: "So, it's just alright?"

Carl: "Sight is the most acute sense we have. I can see all the colors that humans see, but with greater vividness and a more stark differentiation between similar colors. On the bird scale its hawks, falcons, and than us."

Slim Danny: "So you're third on that list?"

Carl: "Yes, technically I am. But I can talk like a motherfucker. Hawks can't say shit, bro."

Slim Danny: "No need to get defensive. I'm just trying to establish what your eyesight is like to understand what you did and did NOT see that day. That's all."

Carl: *"I saw your client clear as day shoot me right in the fucking chest trying to end my life. What more do you want?"*

Slim Danny: *"I want some clarity of what you really saw that day or think you might have saw. According to the recent study in the African Herald, parrots can only see a certain amount of distance before they go airborne and try to get an overhead view."*

Carl: *"You can't believe anything you read in the African Herald. It's literally just a black guy named Harrold who writes about bird watching. He has no idea what he's talking about."*

Slim Danny: *"And you're a parrot giving testimony in a murder trial. How many feet was the defendant in front of you when you allegedly saw him shoot you in the chest?"*

Carl: *"My feet or human feet?"*

Slim Danny: *"Either or is fine. How ever a parrot measures distance. Just give me a general estimate."*

Carl: *"I don't know. Our species doesn't really count like that. We don't measure distance. It's more like, hey man, there's that bird feeder over there, let's just fly over and eat those seeds."*

Slim Danny: *"So would it be a fair assessment to say you rely on your nose more than your eye sight?"*

Carl: *"No!"*

Slim Danny: *"To go to sleep at night, your master has to put a blanket over your cage to trick you into thinking it's dark outside. Isn't that true?"*

Carl: "What? No! It is dark outside! The blanket is for—well, it's there for—is it really not dark outside?"

Slim Danny: "Sadly, no. It's a mental trick us humans use to make you go to sleep. Now that you know that, is it possible your mind was playing tricks on you the day you were shot?"

Carl: "No, I saw what I saw. That man raised his pistol and aimed it at my chest... I think."

Slim Danny: "You think? No further questions your honor."

Judge: "Let's adjourn here for the day."

A hush falls over the courtroom as we leave. I fucking told you Danny was the best. Even against a piece of shit bird. I eye-fuck the shit out of him as the bailiff wheels him out from behind the witness stand. As he nears my table, I stick my foot out in the aisle stopping the wheelchair.

"Say hi to your owner for me. Oh that's right, you can't because she's fucking dead and shit."

"I hope you rot in there you son of a bitch!" Carl responds.

I pull out a wad of hundreds from my pocket and slip it to the bailiff. "Take the parrot to the corner of Greenwich and Barrow, number twenty-five. There's a rich elderly gay couple there that has a bird fetish. Carl, you'll be frozen half dead only to awake inside another man's asshole where you'll have to claw your way out night after night until you die. Enjoy."

The bailiff looks at my lawyer frozen in shock. "Joe the Boss would appreciate the gesture," Danny says with a confident wink.

"Yes sir," the bailiff responds.

I release my foot so he can wheel the parrot out of the courtroom. "You should have flown away, fuckface."

"I'm in a body cast!"

"At least it will make the insertion go a little easier for you," I say flipping him off.

Closing arguments came the following day, with both sides arguing over what a goddamn bird said he saw. I thought I was in clear and so did Danny, but the jury ended up deliberating for three days before finally returning with a verdict. There's no way I could be sent to prison for manslaughter with the only key witness being a parrot, right?

"All rise. The jury has made a decision," the judge says.

As the jury is led into the courtroom, none of them make any form of eye contact with me. My mind races. Is this a good thing? Are they afraid of me? Or are they ashamed at their decision? Is the jury hung like me? I had so many questions as the bailiff took the verdict over to the judge who reads it to himself before handing it back to him.

"You got nothing worry about," Danny says to me as he slaps his hand on my knee.

The jury foreman looks down at the verdict one more time before looking back up at the judge. "All of you have reached this decision on your own?"

"We have your honor. We the jury find the defendant, Saint James Street James, guilty of murder in the first degree."

"What! Are you fucking fisting me? You believed a parrot?" I lash out in anger.

My whores pass out on the ground as if they were shocked by cattle prods while it was raining. The judge bangs his gavel over and over to regain control. The weird girl fights her way through the crowd and lunges over the top of the barrier to grab my cock one last time. The bailiff tears her away like a methed out koala.

"Order in the court! I demand order Goddamnit!" he screams as he continues to bang the gavel.

The crowd finally calms down, as I tense up like a turtle taking a shit. The judge looks at me and asks me to stand. Danny nods, as I readjust my tie and stand up with my hands folded in front of me. He takes his glasses off and rubs his eyes.

"In all my years of being a judge, I can honestly say I've never seen a murder trial like this. Typically, when a man is convicted of murder in the first degree, it requires me to hand you a mandatory life sentence. However, due to the unusual circumstances in this case, I have a hard time giving you a life term… so I'm going to split the difference. A man like you probably has forty years left to live, so I'm going to give you twenty years behind bars."

"Twenty years over a bird's testimony, your honor?"

"You want the rest of your life, son?" The judge asks, starting to get pissed.

Danny yanks on my arm pulling me back into my chair. "No your honor, we are grateful for your ruling."

"Swell. I hear by sentence Saint James Street James to twenty years in the federal penitentiary in Ossining, New York with parole eligibility after ten years. Court is adjourned," he says as he slams down his gavel and leaves the courtroom.

I sit dejected in my chair staring straight ahead as cameras bulbs flash repeatedly in my face. Truthfully, I barely notice that they are even there. It was starting to sink in that I was going to Sing Sing, one of the worst prisons in the United States, and there was nothing I could do about it. Saint James Street James had hit rock bottom... *almost.*

A newsboy suddenly runs into the courtroom frantically, screaming at press row out of breath. "You guys aren't going to believe it! The stock market just crashed!"

There it is. Now I had hit rock bottom completely. Not only was I going to jail, but I was completely broke. The magic of the "Roaring 20's" had come to a grinding halt, and so did my lifestyle. I lit up a heater and exhale as I stare at the ceiling while the reporters pepper me with questions. For the first time, I didn't have any answers, and I didn't have anyone to turn to. Literally. Slim Danny vanished faster than a fart in the wind. That's showbiz, baby. Like I said, the party continues on with or without you. I understood it, but it still didn't make it sting any less.

The bailiff cuts through the reporters and nods, indicating he wants me to stand up. I didn't put up a fight. What's the use? I did it. I fucking killed those people. No one chose to to do this but me. It was time to face the music. As he put the cuffs on me and led me out, that weird chick made one last power grab for my cock. I was appreciative of it. In that particular moment, it meant a lot.

If you recall, at the top of this book, I said the day prohibition started was the second worse day of my life. Today, October 29th, 1929 was the absolute fucking worst. I was I headed to the clink to do hard time and I was now "Mexico poor." If I would have had my pistols on me, I would have ended it right here in the courtroom. No fucking doubt.

Chapter 10
SHOWING MY FUCKING DOMINANCE

S
hit *really* started to set in riding in the back of this gray goose shackled from head to toe as we pulled in to Sing Sing. This wasn't the adobe mud house jails from the Wild West where a couple of drunk cowboys or fat bean dips resided for a few months before being hung in the town square, this was motherfucking prison holmes. Steam rises up from the ground somehow making the sky look more bleak than a fall afternoon in Cleveland. Sing Sing looked like a place where albinos would vacation to avoid even the slightest hint of the sun, and now this is where I will be spending the next 20 years of my life. Fuck me.

You could smell the fear on the rest of these shitbirds on the bus as we enter the gates and pull into this concrete hellhole. The scene was straight out of every stereotypical prison movie when we were shuffled inside for our body inspection. You could hear the roar from the inmates bouncing off the walls on the inside shouting out your stock standard newbie prison phrases.

"Welcome fishes!" one inmate screamed.

"I can't wait to be inside of you!"

"I'm going to ride you like an 18th century bike!"

"The teachings of the honorable Elijah Mohammed are something prisoners believe in!"

"I want you to wear my pants on your face!"

I could see grown men literally shaking in front of me, scared out of their mind. One fat dude even started peeing down his own leg, followed by a hot nervous poot. Here's your first rape vic in here. Me personally, I was more annoyed than anything.

Look, I didn't have any misconceptions about what prison life was like. I knew it would suck, so I was resigned to the fact. The drugs would be stepped on and a lot shittier than the quality I was used to, and I wouldn't be able to bang whores. My conjies wouldn't be allowed here either. That was the one thing that got to me the most. When you're used to crushing the amount of pussy I was slaying on a daily basis, some would even say it's harder than getting off drugs. This would be my biggest mental challenge.

A huge Caucasian guard in his early 40's smiles as he walks up to unshackle my chains. He spins them around his index finger with the same shit eating grin as the deputy in Coloma, California had done when I was locked up there back in the 1850's. This could only mean one thing; he knew who I was.

"Look at who we have here boys! We got a celebrity in our midst. Mr. Saint James Street James," he said as he slowly begins to clap.

The others guards stop checking my fellow newbie inmates to look up. "I know you. You fucked my wife at one of your parties," another guard blurts out.

"I probably didn't pull out either," I respond.

"You're a long way from that penthouse aren't you?"

I smile warmly at him as he undoes my bracelets. "Just out of curiosity, is that key bigger than your dick or about the same size?"

He gave the classic fat man's laugh followed by, "Well, we're about to see how yours measures up in a second. Hope you're not *shy*. Drop'em," he says motioning to my dress pants with his night stick.

"Gladly. This is about to be the best day of your life and the reason why you won't be able to look your wife in the eyes when she asks how your day was tonight when you get home."

I rip off my shirt and kick off my shoes, before pulling down my pants—unleashing the *Hogfather*. As the ninth inch hit the side of my left thigh, the prison staff braced themselves like they were on the tram at Universal Studios that had just been jolted into the water on the *Jaws* ride. One guard even gasped and tried to clutch an invisible set of rosary beads like a Latino grandmother at her nephew's funeral.

"Jesus," the guard said as his laughter quickly escaped his skull.

"This is the closest you'll come to seeing actual wildlife in the Amazon river, amigo," I said as I flung it back against my right thigh making the sound of a wet seal's tail hitting a wooden dock before making it's way back into the water.

"Keep moving he said," trying to make eye contact to avoid meat gazing me even more.

One guard begins to put my clothes into a bag, the next one put his hand on my chest and motioned for me to turn around. I knew this one too. They wanted to see my corn pocket.

"Bend over and spread your cheeks," he said firmly.

"You looking for King Solomon's gold? If so, you're going to have to go deeper."

"I have a feeling there's going to be a lot of treasure hunters eager to get in here soon enough," he said with sarcasm as he jammed two fingers into my ass.

"You obviously don't fucking know me," I replied.

"The 'No Homos' will real soon," he said as all the guards laughed.

"Who are the 'No Homos?'" I asked.

"Just a bunch a guys who like to fuck other dudes and whisper 'no homo' into your ear as they cum. They're going to love you. Delouse this motherfucker, shower him up, and put your pretty new jumpsuit on. Welcome home," he said as he hands me a set prison clothes and bedsheets.

The delousing shit was the equivalent of someone throwing a handful of Gold Bond into your face followed by the quickest cold shower in recorded history. When I put my prison threads on and walked into gen pop, I felt like Russell

Crowe stepping into the Gladiator Ring for the first time. People were screaming at the top of their lungs, throwing ripped out book pages and burnt toilet paper from the second and third floors. It was pure chaos.

A group of older Italian mobsters on the third floor looked down and nodded at me, acknowledging who I was and that I wasn't a fucking snitch. Not being a snitch wasn't good enough in a place like this though. My rep alone wasn't going to keep me safe. I knew I had to flex on motherfuckers or guys would be trying to get me to hold their exposed pockets. That for damn sure wasn't happening. Instead, I drop my bed sheets on the floor and take off my shirt, before cracking my neck side to side.

"Who are the No Homos?" I yell out.

A crew of about twelve ripped gay dudes begin to form a circle around me. The biggest one, a white guy in his mid forties, Joshua Anthony McClurg, pushes through the circle and gets about a foot from my face. (I'll never forget his full government name and neither will you in a minute.) These weren't like the gay dudes you see on reality shows and shit, these were violent motherfuckers who had nothing left to live for and weren't feeling a warm hole from a loved one anytime soon, so they were determined to fuck every weak man who rolled through here… except for one. McClurg sizes me up and smiles.

"You looking to join?" He asks.

"What are the requirements?"

"We all get to take a turn on you, then we'll decide if we want you to suck our dicks afterward—

Crack!

I knock him out cold with a right hook. Everyone looks stunned. The rest of the "No Homos" take a step back as I take off my pants. You could hear a mosquito queef in here. The Italian mobsters nod to the guards, who in turn don't do anything. Now pants-less, I stare down the "No Homos" as I mean mug the shit out of them with their leader laying unconscious on the floor.

"I don't like the fucking terms. If any one of you bitches look in my direction, I'll put every last inch I have inside of you, including both of my balls. You'll be shitting blood through a spaghetti strainer for three years before your asshole recovers. If you don't believe me, you can ask him when he gets out of the hospital next month."

I spit in my hand Heath Ledger style in *Brokeback* and rub it into my cock before flipping McClurg over. With one yank, I rip his pants down to his thighs and mount him. Everyone audibly gasps as I begin raping this man like a fucking wild animal out in the jungle. Every vein was flexed in my neck as I kept blasting out this man's asshole. A few inmates got sick and started throwing up, some turned away in fear, and a few returned back into their cells in disgust.

I wasn't fucking this man out of pleasure, I was fucking him out of dominance. Out of survival. Everyone who's been on the inside and comes out usually gives you the advice of, "Take the baddest man down and no one will fuck with you", or some bullshit version of that. Sometimes that works, but I didn't feel like fighting for the next twenty years in here just in case it didn't. This act of violence I was committing would scar everyone within these walls forever and ensure that I would never be touched. *Ever.*

With each thrust I began grunting even harder so my noises would reverberate off the cement walls and live inside everyone's heads for the remainder of their sentences. It had to exist in the mind of every man in this prison for the rest of their days. I want to have it play over and over in their psyche like the crescendo at the end of the Beatles song *A Day In The Life.*

After 52 minutes straight, I was finally building toward my own crescendo. Yeah, I went a full 52. Let that sink into your mind. Good luck trying to shake that thought when you pull out the driver on the first hole at Pebble Beach on your next "guys weekend" trip. When I came, I screamed out to the prison with every ounce in me—

"NO HOMO!"

I can't be sure because I didn't check, but I would venture to say I pumped 23 ounces of semen into that man. More than one full pound. When I finally pulled out and stood up, blood was all over my dick and his asshole was destroyed. He was bleeding so profusely, it's a miracle he was still alive. The last remaining inmates who were still looking on begin vomiting uncontrollably. *Got'em.* I look each and every one of those motherfuckers in the eyes that was still able to stand there... and then I take a clumpy horse-like shit on this guy's bare back. I grunted every bit as hard as I came too. The other inmates needed to hear it.

"You think I'm fucking done?" I yell out to the now silent prison. "Not a fucking prayer!"

I reach down and rip a huge chunk of hair out of the back of his head and fucking eat it in front of everyone. Yeah. I know, sick shit. You eat someone's hair and you should be committed. Game. Set. Match. I owned these motherfuckers mentally in here now for the rest of my sentence.

No one would ever forget this. You fuck with Street James; you get the worse three-piece combo of your life. That was the message I was poppin' off. How do you explain this after you leave the joint? You can't. That long game was what I was after. You get a stretch like mine, you need a story and a moment that would be talked about forever. I know what you're thinking, how could I personally do this?

Mentally, I had gone to another place. This was the most fucked up thing I have ever done in my entire life. I don't know if I would be sitting here today though if I hadn't done it. When you're in a cage with gorillas you find out who you really are, and I was not the ape to fuck with. This is the only man I've ever been ass inside of in my entire life. I'm not proud of it, but instinctually I had to do it. I spit on his back as the guards slowly begin to walk over.

"One month in solitaire, Saint James," the guard said to me in a somber voice as he and another guard quietly escort me out.

I didn't fight them. I actually wanted them on my side the remainder of my time in here. In a weird way, I had earned their respect too. Seeing some shit like that fucks a man up deep down. Let's face it, this is every man's biggest fear in this life, and they had just witnessed 52 straight uninterrupted minutes of it with a side of potato salad. To this day, every inmate prays he doesn't get "McClurgged" in prison. The guards tell that story at every form of jail in the country to all the newbies coming in.

When we get to solitaire the guards hand me a fresh set of clothes before locking the cell door behind me. Hearing that door shut for the first time really drove home the fact that I was in prison… *for the next twenty fucking years of my life*. It was dark, colder than the other side of an Apple TV remote, and worst of all—I could smell that other man's asshole parts on me as I laid down on my bed. Welcome to Sing Sing.

Unlike most people, I actually enjoyed the fucking hole. The darkness allowed me time to think and sleep in. Let's face it, I've never been a morning person in this life anyway, and in here—I could sleep as long as I want. There were no delusions of grandeur that I was going to dig my way out of this place. These walls were staying put.

I was resigned to the fact that I was going to be up in this bitch for awhile and twenty was pressed right up against my mental gate. Everyone has a mental gate of how much time they can serve without offing themselves, something that separates you from the rest of your thoughts of whether it's worth it to continue living. Twenty years was my personal max. Anything past that, it's bed sheets from the top bunk son. These grimy motherfuckers in here serving life who are getting GED's sound great in a Telluride doc, but in real life, what are you going on for? To live out 40+ years of a horrific existence on the government's dime to eat shitty food, hang out with even shittier people, all so they can send your carved soap chess pieces back to your kids on the outside after you die? They never wanted to be associated with you anyway. Fuck that.

Twenty I could deal with, so I decided to stick it out. Day and night I worked out like Rudy Reyes preparing for *Generation Kill* in my cell, so that when I got out, I was fresh. I had to be yoked like baseball bat to a rooster's egg. It was important to show that not only has the hole not changed me, it made me stronger. I still needed to assert my dominance and let motherfuckers know that my time spent down there didn't affect me. More importantly, if they tested me, I'd be more than happy to go back as far as the others were concerned.

"Street James, time's up," one of the guards says as I do aggressive bed dips.

"You're interrupting my dips. I got one more set of 85," I reply as I blast the shit out of my tri's.

"Sorry," he said as he nods and waits patiently. Of course he fucking waited. After the man rape slash dump out, this motherfucker wasn't saying shit. When I was finished, he escorted me out—almost nervous to cuff me. He looked at my shirt on the bed that I intentionally left behind.

"You want to put your shirt on?" He asked.

"No. I won't be needing it for twenty years. Cuff me up and let's roll out," I said as I voluntarily gave him my wrists.

"People are pretty shook up over what you did."

"Which part? The anal rape or that thunder shit?"

"Both, sir. I don't think you'll have any more problems in here. The warden gave you a cell to yourself in fear of what you might do to another inmate."

"Probably a smart idea. Chances are I'd be wearing my celly's skin like a shawl on an Upper East Side Jewish woman in her late 70's on a fall afternoon."

"Jesus, that is graphically detailed."

"You want small talk, go whisper into a fucking mouse hole."

"You're right. I'm sorry," he says as he puts his head down and picks up the pace.

I told you. You get your rape game strong and motherfuckers get in line faster than the weekly bread drop in Iraq. If you're going to spend 20 in the pokey, the last thing you want is a chatty roommate trying to stranglebate beneath you who regales you with stories of how he almost got away with a B&E that would have put him on "Easy Street". Tell it to the other ex-con employees on break at the local Home Depot in the "Gardening" section after you get out. I don't need that bullshit in here.

Truthfully, I didn't want a cellmate. Period. If you have a cellie, you have to worry about cleaning out your sink after you shave and brush your teeth. Then you have to shit as fast as you can so it doesn't stink as to not offend anyone. You also have to hang a sheet over the bars to just to beat off in peace. Nope. I spread eagle jack where I please, take longer deuces than a quadriplegic, and my sink looks like the trash can inside of an abortion clinic. Anyone who treats their cell like their home probably wants to be there anyway. I treated mine like an AIRBNB in Burma.

As I pass the other inmates for the first time since my rectal obliteration, each one nodded out of respect, silently telling me with their eyes that they would never fuck with me. The "No Homos" wouldn't even make eye contact out of fear that one of them might be next. I made sure to clear my throat as loudly as I can when I pass by, before screaming in their faces—

"ANYONE ELSE LOOKING FOR DICK, BECAUSE I COULD SURE TAKE A SHIT RIGHT NOW?" I say as I slowly bird-dog them as I walk by. Not a single one of these cocksuckers look up as I smile. "That's what I thought, pig dicks."

The prison guard politely guides my arm forward to my cell. I could even sense his fear too, but I oblige and keep on moving. When I walk into to my single bedroom Shangri-La, I was greeted with a piping hot plate of spaghetti with a noted folded next to it. I look at the guard puzzled.

"What the fuck is this? You trying to poison me? I'll feed you your own dick skin from the leftover circumcision you had as a child. I'll find the doctor who performed your procedure. I got people on the outside."

The prison guard retreats. "No, it's from the boys upstairs on level three. They wanted to welcome you here and let you know you'll be well protected for the remainder of your stay."

I nod at him as if I wasn't impressed. "They send down any wine? I can't enjoy a meal without some Chianti."

"Check the toilet. The wine is as fresh as it possibly can be. Real earthy tones that compliment the—

"Shut the fuck up," I say as I see a fermented sock hanging out of the porcelain. "It's in a fucking toilet. Let's not pretend that the grapes were pulled in the early fall after 9pm to ensure the sugar concentration was at its peak. As long as I can pull a relatively decent buzz, I'll take it. Will that be all?"

"Um, yes. Unless you need anything else sir?"

"I'm assuming Parmigiano-Reggiano cheese is probably out of the question, so you can

take your dumb dick the fuck out of here."

Homeboy was so frightened that he gave me a half salute like he forgot the front desk guy's name at his local gym on the way out, before shutting the cell door. As soon as he was out of sight, I sit down on the bed and devour the plate faster than Joey Chesnut. It had been a while since I had a decent meal in my belly. Keeping it one hundred, I was so full afterward, I grabbed the sock full of toilet wine and lay back on my bed sucking on it like a baby cow sucking milk straight from his mom's teet. After 30 days in solitaire, this shit hit me like your first Four Loko during freshman orientation at Arizona State.

The following morning, I took a shit reminiscent of a contestant who just won a reward challenge on *Survivor*. Apple, followed by a milkshake, brohan. The kind that gives you the chills and your calves instinctively flex. I didn't bother to flush immediately either, I wanted that stink to waft through jail like a paper mill just had it's grand opening. I'm now breaking every rule I can simply for effect at this point. A different prison guard approached my cell and immediately recoiled, pulling his shirt over his face. I stonewall this fucking gimp, never breaking eye contact.

"Can I help you?" I ask with more than a hint of annoyance.

"The Genovese family wants to see you… when you're done, obviously."

"Tell them to give me that spaghetti strainer they made this meal with. This is going right through it."

He looked at me confused. "Is that a real question?"

"No. The grates might be too big on that thing. I could probably use a 1/20th gold sifting sieve prospector's pan for a small fresh water stream. Whatever is exiting my butthole right now is that finite. Would you mind ripping off a sleeve on your guard uniform and giving it to me? I'm going to need to go clean the inside of the wheel well here."

He looks at me stunned. "Are you serious?"

"As an 8-year-old's exposed calf to a pit-bull. Sleeve me, honch."

The guard starts awkwardly ripping the sleeve off his arm before handing it to me through the cell. He looks around to see if anyone is watching him and possibly contemplating what the repercussions might be. I start snapping my fingers in front of his face like he's a blind girl wondering which direction to tap dance in. He quickly stuffs the sleeve through the cell as I finally stand up from the toilet. I grab his torn off shirt sleeve and begin wringing it back and forth through my brethren[5] in what is known as the "ole picket fence" maneuver.

The guard looks at me in shock and horror as his sleeve slides through my ass cheeks, taint, and nutz with the speed and precision of a bowler using a microfiber towel to clean an oil ring off his ball to provide more hook. I hold my head skyward throughout in a power move, obviously indicating that I had no intention of making this a quick endeavor. A couple other guards begin to chat in the distance as they approach. Homeboy starts freaking the fuck out, pleading with me.

"Saint James, I need my sleeve back right now," he said through gritted teeth.

"Well, I'm going to need another five passes through. This one is really stingy today. If I don't get the proper follow through down there, I could potentially die of dysentery."

"That's not how that works—

---

5   Brethren is the loving name I have given my penis, balls, and taint. It encompasses the entire area.

"It is goddmanit! Man there's a lot of marinara in here, I'm going to need you on this last pull through."

"WHAT???"

"Tug this through the mud," I say as I hand him the wrist part of his sleeve. "Now, I want you to go slowly. We have only one more shot at this before the others come," I say as I motion in their direction.

"Fine," he says resigned.

"Now on the count of 43, go easy. A quick tug could give me a taint burn, and we don't want that. One, two—

"Hurry the fuck up—

"43!"

He delicately pulls his shirt through my ass and taint like he's trying to save a newborn from quick sand. Once the sleeve was removed, I notice it was covered in mud like Day 3 of Woodstock. Oh well, that's his fucking cross to bear. He quickly pulls the sleeve back over his arm as the other two prison guards walk up. They stopped and look at him strangely, examining his sleeve.

"Jesus Bill, did they make you clean out the soft serve in the cafeteria or something?" He asked with a huge belly laugh.

"Sort of," Bill says with a fake smile.

The other guard sniffs the air. "It smells like shit, Bill."

"It was old Rocky Road. That's why it has all these chunks in it."

Just as he says it, a brown marsh mellow falls off of his shirt and hits the floor.

"I'll be back tonight to get you for your meeting, Saint James."

I look at him not knowing what the fuck is going on, but I nod my head forward in acknowledgement that I'll be there. Whatever the fuck it was, it was better than sitting in this cell all day. I'm not sure what the guard did with that dookie sleeve, nor did I care. What I did know, is that if there's an illegal card game happening later that night, it had to involve the Genovese family—and I was all for it. Anything to make my stretch easier in here was fine by me. Later that night, the same guard came by and grabbed me at my cell, this time without the shitty sleeve.

"What did you do with that brown surrender flag you were wearing?" I asked with a chuckle.

"I washed it in the sink. My wife will sew it back on tonight."

"Good. If we're going where I think we're going tonight, I might need it again tomorrow. It was like the seven dwarfs trying to use a band saw this morning. Let's just hope the food is better," I say as he leads me out of the cell.

Since "lights out" was technically well over an hour ago, the prison was pretty dark at this point. I couldn't really see that well, but the sounds and smells of Sing Sing were alive and well. You know how most evenings east of the Mississippi the nights are filled with the harmony of cicada? Well, here it was the sounds of constant snoring and night poots. Imagine this many low class motherfuckers eating the same disgusting food day after day sharing toilets with bad plumbing? To this day, the atmospheric scent is unmistakable. I can still smell it on a hot July night when I inhale off a joint. Smell is our most powerful sense for a reason. Christ.

Once we cleared the last cell block, I was led through the cafeteria and into the kitchen area to a card table set up in the back by the sinks. One single overhead light irradiates the entire room. Through the thick clouds of cigar smoke I can make out the faces of the older Italians who lined the top floor of the prison when I arrived. They smile and laugh as I walk in. The guard removes my cuffs and walks out as I sit in the lone empty seat at the table. One of them hands me a cigar and a match, which I strike off the table.

"How was the bolognaise we sent?"

"It was great. The gesture is very much appreciated."

"I bet it went right through you like expresso through a midget," he said as everyone laughed.

The tension was broken. "Yeah, I was sifting for gold upstream today, that's for sure," I said with a chuckle.

"Your digestive system will return to normal soon enough."

"You guys eat like that all the time in here?"

"Every day. The mob is powerful in here. These guards work for us, not vice versa. Remember that. We're the reason their kids can afford to go to college. Joey has got you taken care of in here. You didn't rat, and he won't forget it."

I nod understanding. "What happens if Joey gets clipped?"

"Kid, they'll all get clipped eventually. Even though we all come from different bosses, we're all the same family in here. We have to stick to our own. Got it?"

I take a large pull of the cigar and exhale. "Got it. Deal me in."

He playfully slaps the back of the guy's head next to him. "You heard the man, deal him in."

"Okay, okay. By the way, that was some of the most ruthless shit I ever seen on someone's first day in. I don't know how you did it."

"I thought of Herbert Hoover's wife," I say with a straight face.

There's a long pause, before the entire table erupts in laughter. "Get the fuck out of here! That's the ugliest woman I've ever seen!"

"So says you, Tommy! I'd do it," the smaller Italian says.

"We all know you'd do it Tommy, you fucking dirt bag!"

This elicits even stronger laughter. As the cards are dealt, I look around at the faces of these men laughing and suddenly feel more at ease with my situation. Was Sing Sing fun? Not by any stretch of the imagination. Was it tolerable? With these gang of criminals, yes, it was. It turns out there is some honor among thieves when you don't snitch on the ones you work with. It forms a unique bond that most men aren't strong enough to handle. Most men fold at the first hint of adversity. These guys didn't and neither did I.

"Anyone have any coke?"

One of them pulls out a small baggy and throws it down in the center of the chips. "We got everything in here!"

I smile as I dip a pinkie into the bag. The laughter had to have echoed through the entire prison. I'm sure everyone hated us, but what the fuck could they do about it? Answer: not a goddamn thing.

Chapter II
STAMP YOUR FORMS SONNY

December 7th, 1941

I lay in my cot reading the ancient teachings of Socrates desperately trying to figure out how to apply them to my life when a guard suddenly opens up my cell with a skeleton key. He looks at me surprised before asking if he should come back later. Probably because that Socrates bullshit never happened, and I was spread eagle on the bed with my thighs oiled up jacking off into an old pinto bean can just to see if I could do it. He begins coughing loudly out of awkwardness hoping I would stop. Not a goddamn prayer. I was hell bent on achieving a decent climax no matter what. It's important to have goals in this life and to not let anything get in your way, even in prison. Maybe Socrates *did* say that?

"Uh, do you want me to come back later?"

"I'm good, what's up holmes?" I said as I make eye contact mid-stroke.

"Today is your parole hearing. It's time to go down in front of the board—

"In five, four, three, two, one—I didn't even blink my eyes as I shot a fresh load into the back of the can. The first shot sounded like a BB gun connecting with a freshly printed license plate.

"Jesus Christ man."

"He can't stop this," I say as I fill up the rest of the can like it was Campbell's extra chunky clam chowder. When I finish I tuck my dong back into my pants and hop up faster than Charlie's piece of shit Grandpa in *Willie Wonka* after he got that goddamn ticket. I didn't bother to rinse my hands and instead opted for the old "we're bros and we both have dicks" wink.

You might be asking yourself, "Saint James, why weren't you happy for the opportunity at possible freedom?"

Because I wasn't fucking getting it. I knew what I did, and more importantly, who I did it to—and they weren't letting me out of the clink anytime soon. This was strictly a dog and pony show, with the pony being my cock. I wanted to walk in half hard so the parole board could see it slap against my thighs through my boxer-less drawstring pants. Sometimes it's about the mental victories that no one sees. It's the same reason I used to go into rescue shelters and visit the "bigger dogs section" with a pound of shredded turkey meat taped inside my jeans. The dogs would freak out, I would tell the shelter people they were just too dangerous to adopt, and they would usually put them down. I'm sure I saved a life along the way.

This day ended up being completely different, however. Little did I know it would be one of the darkest days in

American history, and one of the brightest periods in my life. As I was ushered in, another guard quickly sits me down into a cold metal chair. When my tater tots hit that seat, I immediately lost wood. A man in his late 60's with wire-rimmed glasses opens my folder containing my rap sheet. He scans it quickly and looks over to a woman next to him in her 40's. She barely makes eye contact with me, which scares the shit out of me. Have I lost it? Have I become George Clooney post *Syrianna* when he did a bunch of shitty movies, got married, and started winking as he told Dad jokes on the red carpet? Does one even know when that actually happens to you as a man in this life?

"Your record says that you're in for bootlegging and mob activities. Would you say that's correct?" He asks in a quiet tone.

"That sounds relatively accurate. Some would say that I was a forceful leader in the community—

"Whatever. Don't care," he says as he quickly scans through the rest of my papers.

"How old are you?" The woman asks looking down at my file.

"Yeah, there is no actual birth date listed in the file, which is extremely rare," he says double checking my file.

"I believe inside my heart that I am thirty-five years old, sir," I reply.

"What does that mean? You don't know your *actual* age?" He asks.

"No sir. My parents died on the Titanic shortly after giving birth to me. It's all strictly a best guess sitch at this point."

"Your mom physically gave birth to you on the Titanic?" The woman asks in shock.

"That's what the Coast Guard wrote on a chalk board when they found me three years later. The orphanage couldn't confirm it," I say as I shrug my shoulders.

Obviously this was a lie. People would have freaked the fuck out if they knew my actual age at that time. Shit, they'd freak out now. There were no records recovered from that goddamn boat sinking back then, so I went with it. I was actually able to ride with that lie for a good fifty years. The pussy I got from it was incredible.

"What did you do for three years at sea?" The man asks incredulously as he takes off his glasses and sets them down on the table.

"I just simply survived. Babies are resilient, especially me. I taught myself how to fish and extract salt from ocean water in order to stay hydrated."

"At three years old? You poor soul," the woman says as she covered her mouth.

I sheepishly looked at the ground. "I'm no victim though, that wooden door was more than enough for my tiny body to shiver around on."

"Would you say that you're healed?" The man asks solemnly.

"No. The constant sunburns likely caused some form of cancer, so I'm more than likely living with some form of melanoma."

"I meant, do you think you've healed in here? Enough to be on the outside and contribute to society?" He asks.

"Oh yes sir. I sure have."

He peers over to the rest of the board and shakes his head. At this point I was fully expecting him to tell me to go fuck myself and the guards would escort me back to my cell, but clearly he had other things on his mind. Before he could say a word, a set of loud airplanes roared overhead above the prison. The man looks out the window, before leaning over the desk with his hands folded.

"How would you feel about going to war?"

"As in *tug a*?"

"No, World War."

"There's another one?"

"Jesus man, do you not know what's going on out there?"

"Not yet. This time of day I usually spend with myself in a long jerk sesh followed by a loose four to five-hour nap. I'm in fucking jail, bro."

"Our country is under attack. The Japanese have bombed Pearl Harbor and we are in desperate need of troops. If we commute your sentence, would you be willing to fight overseas?"

"We would release you immediately and you would be taken directly to boot camp," another man on the parole board says in a serious tone.

I thought about the prospects of fighting in another war, then I thought about how quickly I would be in someone's vagina. It took everything in me to not lick my lips with excitement and stutter like a man with half a tongue. Instead, I compose myself and slowly shake my head forward.

"I would do anything for this country."

"Good, that's all I need to hear—

"I will not let a greasy fucking gook put one yellow foot on United States soil. I will send those slants back to Japan so goddamn quickly you'd think I invented a fucking time machine, and when they return home they'll be a full day younger."

"Ummmm, I said that's all I needed to hear. You may return to your cell to gather your belongings before boarding the bus."

"Oh, I'm cool. I'm not taking chess pieces I've made out of soap or a half roll of toilet paper or any shit like that. Give me the suit I was dropped off in and I'm all set."

"Godspeed," he said.

"I don't know. 4.2 forty, what are you thinking? You think he's faster?"

"Guard, get him the fuck out of my sight."

Deuces Sing Sing. As I was led to the cage to pick up my suit, I was surprised to find the original suit I walked in here with— replaced by a full on Don suit complete with a brand new gold watch from the Dagos. This shit was still inside the fucking bag, that's how fresh it was. These fucking mobsters do shit right. Now look, I certainly didn't like prison one goddamn bit, but man did these motherfuckers make it more enjoyable. I felt a certain kinship amongst these men. Plus, let's face it—the mob ain't going anywhere. I knew I'd see the likes of them again some day.

For some reason all throughout my life, I've gotten along with crooks and rule breakers as opposed to these 9 to 5 dicks kicking back on the barcalounger with a Bud Heavy after work, only to roll upstairs and have angry doggy style sex with their fat wives so they don't have to see their faces. That shit is depressing. Yeah, I might have gone to prison and fucked a dude, but it made me feel more alive than one night of living that minimum wage life. You can keep your change, I want a sack full of diamonds and some cocaine in this life, *holmes*. If it isn't served to me on a tiddy, then I'm disappointed.

As I slip on my watch and tighten the clasps obnoxiously in front of the guard's face, I smile and say, "I'm all set, chief."

"Great. Where to?"

"A whorehouse? I'm buying," I say as I pull a gangster wad of money out of my pocket. I didn't even have to look to know it was there, I felt it brush against my dong when I was putting my pants on. You think the Italians would suit me up and watch me down then *not* leave a fat grip in my pocket to get wet? Fuck off.

"No, I mean what branch of military? There are designated busses to take you to basic training."

"I don't know? Who gets the most pussy?"

"The fly boys," he says as he laughs and points at my new suit. "You'll fit right in. AAF for this one Lewis!" he screams down the hall before giving me a shove in the back toward his direction.

As I walk toward Lewis, the last guard standing between me and the outside, he flings open the door and points me toward a Greyhound bus. I hold my solid gold watch up to block my eyes, because let's face it, nothing fights the bright sun better than fresh gold. I squint harder than that fucking kid in *The Sandlot* as I swallow my first taste of actual freedom in ten years. I'll spare you with the *A&E Locked Up* bullshit, but it really did feel nice. A sharp breeze suddenly picked up and re-brushed my dong against my money, which felt even sweeter.

"Get on the fucking bus Saint James," Lewis yells out.

I nod and shuffle my way over, rubbing my eyes to regain full sight. The door of the bus flung open and an elderly black man nods at me as I go in for a pound. I know, pounding fists didn't exist back then, but I was always racially ahead of my time.

"Where are we headed?" I ask.

"San Antonio," he replies flatly.

"The fucking place where we lost the Alamo? That's not a good fucking omen."

He smiles and laughs. "You ever flown a plane?"

"No," I reply.

"Well that ain't a good fucking omen either," he chuckles. "Sit anywhere you like Capone."

I smirk and take a seat toward the front, because Rosa Parks hadn't done shit yet. Truthfully, I just wanted to be by myself. I saw six or so other ex-cons get on the bus and it seemed like everyone else wanted the same. After being with so many dudes for so long, you want some goddamn space. As the bus hums to life, I let down my window so I could take in the fresh air. The following description below will probably be read by Morgan Freeman in the audiobook, but for you super poor motherfuckers that can't afford it, please read this as him. Let's face it, I'm famous enough that he'll do it.

As the brakes on the bus released, that hard familiar jolt of a large bus leaving for a long journey kicked in. You know that air pressure sound. It's the same one you've heard since you were six years old. I was finally getting out of here. Where I was going or what I was doing really didn't matter. It was still hard to shake the sights and smells of me fucking that man 10 years ago... or thinking about the scent of his asshole parts on my genitalia, but somehow I knew I had to get past it. Was it with senoritas and margaritas in San Antonio? Who knows, but my money is on "probably".

As we drove across this land, the land I had once fought for during the Civil War, it dawned on me that I was about to be brave as shit and protect this land one more time. I'm an amazing human with a vibrant spirit that can never be shook—

As The Sun Rises, It Dawns On Him

"Ya'll gotta shit? Now is the time to do so!" the guard barked out as the bus pulled into a gas station.

I was suddenly jolted from a long slumber. There's no better way to be awoken from the most peaceful sleep you've had in years than by a fat man stretching out the seams on his cheap guard uniform and asking you if you need to evac your bowels at a truck stop shitter. I wipe the sleep crust out of my eyes and exit the bus.

"Where are we?" I ask him.

"Kentucky. Why, you into sight seeing? If so, I can have the driver swing by Mammoth Cave National Park! We could see some stalagmites?"

"That would be lovely, I've never seen them in full—

"Shut the fuck up. Ten minutes to dump out," he says as he taps his watch with his nightstick.

I nod my head and step off the bus, stretching my arms skyward. As I walk in to the convenient store, I see a brochure for Mammoth Cave National Park. The stalagmites did look incredible. Since I had some money, and there was a wait for the restroom, I decide to grab some chips. When I lift a bag off the shelf, I look clear through to the other side where I could see half a face of a beautiful girl in her mid-20's. This chick has long blonde hair that was swept over the other half of her face. She winks at me with a large blue eye. Goddamnit, Saint James Street James still has it. Even after a ten-year stretch in the pokie. She leans over carefully so the clerk, an old man in his early 70's, doesn't see her.

"Hey, you want me to throw you a beej?" she whispers seductively.

I smile politely, hating to let her down. "I can't fit my dick all the way over to your aisle. It would be close, but I'd ultimately fall short."

"No," she giggles. "Meet me in the last stall of the men's room. I'll go first," she says as she saunters off.

This chick was a fucking Roosevelt from behind. No polio. I gave it the standard two-minute warning, then make my way back to the men's room. Once inside, I enter the last stall locking the door behind me—but she wasn't there. Instead, there was a large glory hole cut out in the stall partition with pencil writing above the hole that read: **Stick Yo Dick Here Dummy.**

I lean down and look through the hole where I can see her big blue eye once again wink at me. It was a little different from the glory hole I created during the Wild West, but it was nice to see that my innovation had evolved. I'm sure Benjamin Franklin turned on a fucking light switch one day, then pissed all over his kite in the corner. Genius always prevails.

I unzip my pants and insert my penis into the hole, receiving some of the best oral sex I've had in my entire life. I'm not even saying this from a prisoner stand point of just getting fresh out the joint, having his first suck job from a woman in years. Come on, it's SJSJ brother. No, this beej was special, which was surprising based on her looks. Usually it's the bigger girls who aim to please like this, but home girl was buttering the cobb today. Right as I'm about to climax I hear—

"Engine? You in here?" Come on out, Engine! Goddamnit you better not be in here!" a man yells out.

I peak over my stall and see that it's the old man clerk. He's shuffling along, pushing in the stall doors in one by one with his cane. Shit. Now, I'm in a tough spot here. I'm so close to launch that it would be a shame *not* to get off at this point. Plus, who is Engine? Maybe he was looking for his dog or something. I tried to focus, but his cane suddenly jams her door open, and the old man goes ballistic!

"Engine! Jesus Christ almighty! I told you not to be doing this! Especially in my place of business," he says as he throws his cane on the floor.

"Daddy, I'm sorry. I just want a man to settle down with! You always tell me to find a nice man to have kids and make you happy," she says in a panic.

He cocks a pistol and kicks open my door. I pull my dick out of the glory hole as fast as I can and turn toward him. Maybe it was the gun, or the situation, or how long I'd been on the inside—but I couldn't hold back. I ejaculated all over this old man with what seemed like endless ropes. He was wearing a thin white work shirt and he was now suddenly thrust into a wet t-shirt contest in Fort Lauderdale circa 1983. He was so shocked, as was I, that both of us didn't know what to say. Finally, the girl broke our silence.

"Doesn't he seem like a nice man, daddy?"

The clerk becomes enraged. "He doesn't want to be with you, dumb fool. Who wants to be with a girl who has got half her face melted off by an engine block?"

"What are you talking about man?" I ask in shock.

He flips the other side of her hair out of her face up over the top of her head. It's like fucking Aaron Eckhart as *Harvey Two Face*. To my credit, the half of her face that was exposed really was beautiful... but the other half, well it was all fucked up. Her eye was melted shut, it was bad. This weird moment was thankfully interrupted by the prison guard with his nightstick in his hand, who flings open the restroom door. My pants are down, I'm half hard, and a 70-year-old man is wearing my cum like a villain in *Spiderman*. The guard couldn't help but laugh.

"You want to stay and settle down with your new friends, or do you want to come with us?"

"Is he a prisoner?" The old man asks.

"Used to be. Early release. He's going into the military now if he can put his dick away," he says as he continues to laugh.

"You sure can pick'em Engine!"

"I'm sorry Daddy!" she says as she runs out.

"Let's go Saint James. Zip up and wash your hands," the guard says as he looks at me disgusted.

My boner finally dies down as I casually slide in right by him and wash up. It felt good to empty out my balls near somewhat of a lady mouth again, but I wish it was under different circumstances. Like, I don't know—thinking out loud—if she had both eyes and a full jaw bone. Nothing I could do. You had to be there.

As I walked back on the bus, the guard whispered to me, "Welcome to Kentucky. It will never change."

He was right, it hasn't. It's a strange part of America where rules or common decency don't apply. As the bus fires back up, I look out the window and see Engine waving at me with a crowbar. I laugh like I had taken an edible on a red-eye as a Keanu Reeves drama is playing during the in-flight movie. When the bus starts moving, I give her a salute with two fingers as she grows smaller in the distance. All I could think was, I hope she finds her better half someday. Nailed it.

The one thing that had improved during my time in prison was the transportation system. Roads and highways were actually paved, and more more people were driving cars and buses cross country, rather than trains. Fucking technology, man. As cars whizzed past us, I long for a day where I could take a steed down the coast of California back to Coloma while only stopping to get head with a finger in my ass at a whorehouse midway. Some day. #dreamsandshit

For now, I had to survive yet another war, then figure out how to make some bread in this "new" America and become a goddamn legend again. When the bus finally stopped at base in San Antonio, I could see young men running in groups, doing push-ups, marching—all the shit I fucking despise. Yet here I was, back on this bullshit. Fuck me. Your stereotypical drill sergeant in his early 40's, Lance Whitsaw, climbs aboard when the bus comes to a halt.

"Good afternoon gentlemen. I am Sergeant Whitsaw, and I am the nightmare inside your wet dreams. I will be assuming ownership of your souls for the next eight weeks.

Now men, it's time to leave the comfort of your shit stained granny panties here on the floor and enter the real world!"

I raise my hand to ask a question. "Excuse me, sir?"

"What goddamnit?"

"What is comfortable about wearing and or holding our grandmother's shit stained panties? If anything, we would *definitely* want to leave those behind if we had them in our possession."

The other cons chuckle with laughter, which leaves Sergeant Whitsaw enraged. He walks to the back of the bus and gets right in my face. His face was so red with anger that he resembled an albino sunbathing on the roof of his apartment complex mid-June in Death Valley. A solemn bead of sweat from his forehead hit my thigh as he leans in as close as he possibly can.

"What's the last name of the crime family you came from Dago?"

"Street James, sir."

"Street James? Now what in the hell kind of last name is that?" He asks with laughter as two more beads of sweat shake out into my pants.

Now I'm becoming agitated. "I guess it's instructional if you need the cross road to an address."

"And your first name?"

"Saint James, sir."

The BMI in his face rises an extra hundred points. "Saint James? Were you named after a Catholic Cathedral, or is that where your parents had dropped you off at after seeing how how ugly you were at birth?"

Drip. Another bead of his sweat hits my pant leg like an amoeba hitting a petri dish from an eye dropper. Now I was pissed. Wrong move, *hombre*. I was never really good with authority anyway, this just sealed his fate.

"If one more bead of your pig sweat touches my five-thousand-dollar suit, I will put this white patent leather shoe so deep in your ass, you'd think I was measuring low tide at a southern creek with a yard stick ten feet off the intercostal. We clear?"

He shakes his head in anger. "What the hell did you just say to me?"

"Could you not hear me or are you just that fucking dumb? I bet your family name is Whitsaw, because God took whatever whit he gave you and sawed it in half to give some to your retarded brothers and sisters. Procreation isn't for everyone."

You could see an actual blood vessel burst inside his eye like an overcooked hot dog exploding in a microwave. He was so fucking livid that began to jam is index finger into my shoulder. For me, that was the straw that broke Artie Lange's nose. You don't poke another man with a hard digit in the chest. We both knew what was coming next.

"How about we step off this bus and find out in front of everyone what God *actually* gave me?"

"What's the bet?"

"You won't be alive to collect one after I'm through with you," he gnarled.

"When I am, I want two things. One, I want to skip all of this bullshit," I said as I motioned to the aforementioned dudes who were running around, doing pushups, and crawling through the mud.

"Let me get this straight, you want to skip basic training?"

"Yeah, I'm all good on all this stupid shit. If I wanted to hug dudes and sing songs, I'd roll out in San Fran on a Friday night."

"That ain't happening—

"TWO. I want you to dry clean my suit and put it in my barracks, neatly hung up. I'm sure there's enough sulfate in one of your drops of sweat to cause discoloration for a lifetime on this thing. I'm a made man and we take pride in our suits. Now, if you're as bad ass as you say you are, this should be no problem."

He nods and thinks it over. "And if I win, what do I get?"

"This gold watch. You see my suit, you know this shit is real, and more than likely half your yearly salary. I'm sure the missus wouldn't mind if you pawned it for some extra cash to feed your four to six overweight children that aren't really waiting for you at home. What do you say?"

He pulls his hat off. "Deal, fuckface. Off the bus. The rest of you stay right here until I'm done with this asshole!"

Sergeant Whitsaw turns and powerwalks off the bus immediately. I slowly take off my tie and jacket, handing it to the bus driver before walking off.

"I'll be right back for those," I say to him over my shoulder.

"You got a real set of brass dangling on you, honkey. I ain't never seen no shit like this before," he says as he neatly folds the jacket.

Sergeant Whitsaw and I slowly begin to roll up our sleeves and ball up our fists as we begin to circle one another. Everyone on the bus slams their windows open and moves to the right side so they can see. Other privates stop doing pushups and jog over to check out the show. I obviously take my time so the audience could grow. After three books, you know I like as much gravy on these biscuits as daddy can get.

"You should take off your watch. I don't want anything happening to it before I slap it on my wrist," Sergeant Whitsaw says.

"Don't worry, I'll tell you what time it is in ten seconds."

With that, he lunges at me with a hard jab. I expertly dodge it and catch his arm with one hand up by his elbow, lowering it in the process. With my other hand, I unzip my pants and slang dis dick around his wrist. It wraps around it like a monkey tail around a tree. I look down at my dong and shake my head.

"Is it two o'cock already? The battery must be low; this can't be right? No wonder you wanted a new watch. Having another man's cock around your wrist probably isn't going to give you the preciseness you were looking for."

I thrust my hips and unwhip my dick from his wrist and elbow him in the face as I let go of his arm. All the other privates howl with laughter. He quickly tries to regain his composure, but you can tell he's embarrassed as shit. Also, super important note, my dong is still hanging out of my pants. I just didn't feel like putting it back in. The sunshine feels nice on it. He squeezes his fists even tighter, then charges me.

"You motherfucker!" he screams at me, while running at top speed.

Whitsaw throws a wild haymaker, which I duck, and in turn give him a ruthless body shot to the rib cage. The punch was so intense that he physically threw up all over my dick. I stop and look at the bits of sick all over my pants. Holy shit, man. I was as grossed out as every other private there. Who throws up on another man's ding dong? Savages, that's who. Fuck this guy. As much as I love to put on a show, now I just want a shower. An innocent fight with your cock out had suddenly turned into a gay man's fetish video on the dark web. Time to end this bullshit.

"Goodnight, fuck boi."

I launch a hard uppercut and knock Sergeant Whitsaw damn near three feet off the ground. He lands unconscious in the dirt with a thud and immediately starts snoring like a tranq'd boar. I take off my pants and wipe the puke off my dong, before throwing them down on his unconscious body. The bus driver walks out and puts my jacket around me like I'm James Brown exiting stage left. I nod at him and look toward all the other privates.

"Anyone know where I can take a fucking shower? There's regurgitated MRE all over my cock and balls."

Everyone stares at me in shock. Welcome back to the military.

Chapter 12

I'M LEARNING TO FLY...
INTO PEOPLE.

After knocking out the drill Sergeant, I feel bad waking him up after my shower to ask where the flyboys are, so instead I just peacock over to the planes. Goddamnit if these planes weren't beautiful. No homo. Obviously, I don't want to fuck a plane, but I'd rub my ding-dong on a wing. These are the type of planes that Harrison Ford flies right after he lights up a joint after getting out of bed, before he crashes it an hour later near a residential area. I can't overstate how majestic these things are up close and personal.

I know what you're thinking, "Saint James Street James, do you know how to fly a plane?" *I sure don't.* But that's never stopped me from doing anything in this life. If you're afraid of doing something just because you've never done it, then anal sex wouldn't be so popular would it? Right now I bet you're envisioning the first time you did anal, man or woman, and you remember the surprise of it going in don't you? I bet if you take a deep inhale right now you can probably smell the room you were in. Notice I said "room". That's because no one buttfucks for the first time in a car. It's true. Think about it. It's too hard to maneuver with those kind of nerves.

The first plane I walk up to has a shark's mouth painted on the nose of it. I've always admired the craftsmanship of older American planes and muscle cars. When I hear people say German engineering is the best in the world, I ask them to take the gag ball out of their mouth before continuing to talk. Give me one of these planes and a 71' Plymouth Road Runner any fucking day. If that doesn't get your dick hard, fire up your Prius and let a real man fuck your wife.

"You here to fly it or stroke it?" A good looking white dude in his early 20's says as he smiles and grabs his junk.

"What's your government name?" I ask.

"Greg Hanson. Other pilots call me eight ball."

"Cocaine habit?"

"What? No. I lost a testicle in a lawnmower accident and the doctor replaced it with an eight ball from the local pool hall next door."

"That sounds uncomfortable and rather hard to walk actually."

"It is," he says as looks down at his special shoe that is higher than the other.

"You the guy who knocked out Whitsaw and wants to skip basic training?"

"Indeed I am."

"You might want to rethink that private. I'm sure you ex-cons can handle a pistol, but flying a plane is a completely different beast."

I look through the windows inside the cockpit of the plane. "It doesn't look that difficult. It's just a bunch of shiny knobs like the rest of you assholes."

All the flyboys erupt in laughter. "Just a bunch of knobs, huh? Well hop on in and give her a spin in the sky. I'm sure you'll be fine. The rest of us required nine weeks of training, but that's probably just the military being overly cautious. Get in and let's see what you got," he says as he slaps me hard on the back.

I fire up a heater before climbing inside the cockpit. Let's see, button, button, button, and ignition. The plane roars to life. Everyone stares at me in shock as I pop open a window and ash my heater.

"Yeah, you guys are real fucking hero's," I scream out of the window of the plane.

"Fly it around the base and over those mountains!"

He points to a set of mountains off to my left. I see them and proceed to give him no less than 48 hand gestures, before saluting him. Carefully, I then steer the plane forward and put my head out the window looking around.

"You looking for the runway?" He asks.

"Don't need it. I fly where I fly. But while I'm up there, I'm going to need you to look for my condoms. I think the box fell out of my suit pocket when I kicked the shit out of your Sergeant. They're real important. Lambskin. My great grandfather gave them to me. Look, I never use the goddamn things, but they're sentimental. You understand. See you in few, fuckfaces."

With a final wink and mock blow job motion, followed by my other hand faking another dick entering my face from above and then simulating completion all over my face with both fake dicks, I ease off the brakes and begin steering the plane forward. I didn't bother with the runway when I can see a perfectly good road right in front of me that led into the base. What do you know, just like a pregnant lactation expert, you tug on enough levers and some boobie juice is bound to squeeze out. Same thing with flying. Press and pull anything, you're hugging the friendly skies in no time. The entire base who saw me kick the shit out of the Sergeant earlier cheered like I was Amelia Earhart taking off over the Atlantic. I gave a fist pump to the boys to really get shit poppin' off and escalate my legend.

Once I cleared the base, it was smooth sailing. I fucking flew everywhere around San Antonio. Like an unexpected rim job during a routine HJ, I never knew how much I loved it. *Both* flying AND rimmers bt-dubs. Part of me wondered if I shouldn't just keep going down into ME-HE-CO and call it a day. I didn't want to get stuck in this war the same way I had during the Civil War, but there was one problem—I didn't know how to land. That shit is *way* harder than I thought. ME-HE-CO was out of the question now, but then again, so is staying alive it seems. No wonder we never found Amelia Earhart again.

The only landmark I recognize is the fucking Alamo, which I gave serious consideration... *to crashing into.* We fucking lost anyway, does anyone still give a shit about that place except for border jumping tourists taking "Fuck You

America" pics? I could dive bomb the place and call it a day. Hell, Eisenhower might even build me a goddamn statue in it's place. The only thing that was rough about it was the stone wall around it. I definitely wouldn't survive. We built the shit out of that thing.

Ultimately, I decided that my existence was way too important to sacrifice, and these big ole balls *swanging* between my legs still had plenty of cum to empty out, so instead I pick out the nearest taco cart and crash the fuck through that. What? I need something to slow down my speed. Go to the Wailing Wall in Israel if you want to make a scene and cry about it. I'm important as shit and I need to live... unlike the two people cooking hot dogs, bacon, and onions on the street beneath me. Take a moment and deeply inhale. You can smell it can't you? Those fucking Mexicans sure can cook a damn fine what-ever-the-fuck-those-are-called.

As I guide the plane down with the precision of Muhammad Ali playing a game of *Operation*, I take aim at the cart. The plane skidded in violently like a fat man taking a shit on a small toilet seat at an ocean rental cottage. I obviously lived, but a fifty-year old Mexican dude perished. By "perished" I mean he got chopped up in the propeller faster than parsley during the final ten seconds of a challenge on *Top Chef*. His arms and legs shot off in every direction on a compass as my head bashed off the steering wheel. I was knocked out cold.

The scent of fresh flautas and the sounds of loud clapping finally brought me back to life inside the cockpit.

What the fuck? I look up and see his fat Mexican wife literally clapping fresh uncooked tortillas in her hand back and forth with no emotion. She didn't even seem to be pissed that her husband had been Willam Wallaced all over the street. I felt blood streaming down my forehead as I try to pull myself out of the plane. The woman clapping tortillas back and forth in her hands remains emotionless.

"How long was I out?" I ask.

"Flauta?" She responds in a monotone voice.

"Yes, I see that. It's lovely. How long was I unconscious?"

"You pay. You ruin flauta machine. No more business today," she says pointing to her demolished taco stand.

"I'm assuming that's your last one left?"

"*Si. No more flautas.*"

"You keep saying flauta, but it's still a tortilla until you cook it and roll it up around meat. Look, I love the word too, so how much for your last 'flauta' and your dead husband?"

"*Cinco dollares.*"

I pull out the gangster wad of cash in my pocket, peel off a hundred, and hand it to her. "I'm obviously going to need change," I say as I press the uncooked flauta against my head to stop the bleeding from the crash.

She looks at me hurt and confused. "*Que?*"

The white flour tortilla fills up with blood. "You *Comprende*, so cut the bullshit. A deal is a deal. Five dollars."

"But my husband—

"You didn't give a cat fuck about your husband until I pulled a Benjamin out of my pants and wafted it underneath your beak. Waddle along and bring me back my change before the *policia* get here Maria, and shit starts getting real."

I follow that up with a two finger whistle loud enough to get those tree trunks moving toward a beat up pickup truck where I see two other fat Mexicans shucking corn in the back. With my own blood soaking through the tortilla, I hear an ambulance racing toward me in the distance. I don't bother to get up, because that's what an ambulance is for. I needed drugs ASAP and I knew that ambulance had them. Nothing is better than getting wet with morphine on a Sunday afternoon. Inject first, ask questions later *hombre*.

When the ambulance pulls up, two shocked medics hop out and spot me sitting on the sidewalk next to the downed plane. I wave them over with my blood soaked tortilla. They give me a strange look and that's when I realize that my pants are ripped open and my entire dong is exposed. I don't even bother to try and cover it up.

"Jesus Christ. It's a miracle you survived this crash," one of the medics says as he eyes the wreckage.

"Yeah that's cool and all, but I'm going to need some morphine to deal with the pain right now. Pop your kit open, and let's grip it and rip it, brother."

"Are you hurt anywhere else besides your head sir?" The other medic asks.

"Is your last name Street James?" I ask.

"No," he responds.

"Cool, then you're not my fucking Dad so let's prep that needle chief. I was just in a plane crash, I killed a fat Mexican dude, and my fucking ding dong is exposed. Do I need anymore reasons for morphine, man?"

The medics try not to stare at my dick, which is resting against the concrete curb through the rip in my pants. "Right away sir," they respond as they race back to the ambulance to get the morphine and a stretcher.

I fire up a heater as they run over holding that old bullshit stretcher from back in the day made out of cloth and what looks like a fucking ladder. One of the medics leans down with a syringe to inject me with the morphine and I wave him off. Instead, I take it from him, jam it into my thigh and start the fucking party. They stare at me stunned.

"Sir, do you want to lay down? That's probably a lot stronger than you think and you're going to want to be in a prone position—

"Shut the fuck up. I've been rocking this shit since before you stretched out your mother's sugar walls and entered this earth. I'll lay down after I get my cash."

"I'm sorry? Your cash?"

"Yeah, the big dipper over there owes me change. I'm not leaving without it. This tortilla wasn't free."

"That's kind of ruthless man," one of them replies.

My eyes are too preoccupied on the truck to deal with their judgmental bullshit, and with the morphine kicking in, I just want a completion to this transaction. I two finger whistle at her once more. One of her brothers in the back of the truck holds up an ear of corn as she smiles. Not a prayer. I know this move.

"NO I'M NOT TRADING MY 95 DOLLARS FOR AN EAR OF FUCKING CORN! THIS IS AMERICA. I WANT DINERO. IN MY FUCKING HAND. ANDELE ANDELE E-I E-I –UH-OH. WHAT'S HAPPENING NOW?"

She shakes her head defeated as she waddles back with ninety-five dollars wadded up in her fat hand. Yet again, I know what you're thinking, "Saint James Street James, why do you need the money, you killed her husband?" Fuck off with that shit.

First of all, it's the principal. Second, life just isn't as valued in Mexico the same way as it is here in America. Truthfully, homeboy probably lived five years past his life expectancy before he got diced up like that. Each day after that is considered a gift to these people. All I did was basically tell him there was nothing left under the Christmas tree. I'm sure she'll make a candle out of him, sell it in her village, and make whatever the opposite of a "fortune" is off of it.

Seconds after grabbing the money out of her fat sweaty palm, the morphine hits and I immediately fall off the curb face down into the stretcher and into another dimension. The last ten years in jail really put a dent in my tolerance for synthetic drugs. I'm not a fisherman, but I was fucking *reeling*. It felt great to have that sweet, sweet Morpheus running through my veins again. Fuckin' A, there *really* is nothing better than having hardcore drugs in your system is there?

When the ambulance arrived back at base, I couldn't help but notice the stiff breeze as the doors open and the medics begin to carry me out. Mostly because my dick was still exposed, and morphine generally makes you feel a little chilly. Rule of thumb if you're out there raging this weekend— BRING A HOODIE IF YOU'RE DIPPING A TOE INTO THE OCEAN OF THIS SHIT.

With the bright sun now shining down on my face, my eyes start to flicker as they carry me into the hospital. Nigh nigh. Dreamland son. My game was over and Morpheus had won.

I was awoken hours later to a beautiful nurse standing over me with a sponge, cleaning around the base of my volcano. She looked like one of those pinup girls from Time magazine back in the day, or every girl that lives in Los Feliz today. As she lightly scrubs my body, almost edging my penis, I can't help but see a glint of confusion in her eyes. I slowly reach my hand down and squeeze her wrist.

"Is there something you want to say? Or perhaps a measurement you want to take for your journal?"

"I'm sorry," she says as she blushes and turns away.

"It's okay, I've done this hundreds, if not thousands of times before."

"You have?" She asks with shock.

"Yes. I'm a child of God and I believe in being intimate without ever knowing the person."

"I can see that, it's just so unusual to see something like this," she says finally turning back, staring right down the barrel of my single gage shotgun, aka my penis.

I put my hands behind my head, knowing what's coming next. "Go ahead and give it a tug if you don't believe it's real. I really don't mind."

"Okay," she says as she slowly puts her hand between my legs. As I wait for the Olympic-style hammer toss, I am pleasantly surprised when she goes underneath my carry-on bag. Ah, a lady who knows how to work the ole' prostate—

"WHAT THE FUCK!" I scream.

With one swift motion she pulls out half a hot dog that was apparently lodged inside my asshole. She wiggles it in front of her face and stares in shock. I can hear the semi-cooked dog being thrown down into a metal bed pan on the floor as she recoils in disgust.

"What kind of man are you?"

"The kind who crashed his plane into a hot dog cart. Look, I'm into a lot of crazy shit, but a raw Mexican dog up the poop chute isn't one of them."

"So, you didn't feel that on the entire ambulance ride?"

"No, I was out. I thought I felt a preacher's hand, which I imagine is similar."

"What about the four and half hours you were sleeping in here?"

"Jesus, I've had a hot dog up my ass for five hours? Man, that needle candy *really* hit me. I'm sorry you had to see that. Fuck, I'm sorry I had to live it. I tell you what, just grab that crutch leaning up against the wall and rip a bed sheet in half to make a splint for my dong, and I'll get out of your hair. Also, can you get that hot dog out of here? It fucking stinks."

She smiles sweetly and kicks the bedpan underneath my bed and leans in. "Let's save that crutch for some poor little kid who actually needs it. You seem fine to me."

"Well, I am heading off to war. If you want a child I'll never write to or see, I'm definitely your guy."

"Oh, I think you'll write me back after the special care I'm about to give you."

"No, I definitely won't, because I prefer to speak my thoughts like an adult—but right now I need that beaver."

She pulls the curtain across, dividing the room, as if that's going to make a fucking difference. That's like giving an elephant one drop of Visine after getting mud in it's eye. When I pull out the bagpipe, the world hears it, and this chick is a fucking old school banger. She's a pinup perfect 10, and I'm giving her every last skin cell I have on my shaft. She knows it, I know it, and goddamnit if she doesn't play the part of every hospital nurse fantasy before it became a "thing" to wear baggy scrubs like a genderless pile of shit.

No sir, this was everything you dream it would be. White dress with the white hat and red cross. Siren red lipstick. Eye shadow so blue it would make Picasso blush. She was a rubber glove short of a Blink 182 album cover. And dem tiddies—more pristine than fresh powder on the Swiss Alps.

The reveal was nothing short of awe inspiring. She stood at the foot of the bed and used every last second on the play clock, taking her time to unzip the back of her dress. Any woman that takes that much time teasing out a body reveal like that knows goddamn well what kind of engine she has underneath that hood. Most women are body conscious and fumble around with a quick dress/bra combo over the head maneuver before diving into the bed quicker than an Asian on a high dive. This nurse was presenting herself in slo-mo like she was pulling back the sheet over a bust in Canton, Ohio.

Keep in mind the lighting in a hospital room and show some fucking respect. These are the fluorescents, which look terrible on every single person in the world… except for me and her. She didn't even look over at the light switch once. This kind of confidence was unrivaled from any other woman at the time. Brav-fucking-O.

I was simultaneously nervous and excited at the same time. When the dress finally hit the floor after the zipper came to a stop, I lost my breath like the moment the waiter puts down the sizzlin' fajitas in front of you at Chili's. My eyes welled up a little too. Then the bra came off. I'm sorry, I'm going to need a moment. Let me do a big fat fucking rail of cocaine before I get into the description of these fucking beef cannons. You should too. I'll wait. Call your fucking drug dealer.

LINE UP YOUR COKE RIGHT HERE, THIS IS A PROPER LINE FUCKBOI.

She seductively unclasps the bra with both hands. Her tits release like horses at the starting gate of the *Kentucky Derby*. I almost felt bad for the bra that had to hold those blouse mounds back. That's too much tension and I'm surprised the fabric survived to be honest. They were simply magnificent. It was like seeing Chinese warheads rolling down the street at their military parade. They were so perfect and perky that they didn't see real. Did she sleep wearing waffle cones as a teenager? Unfortunately, I'll never know. It was like seeing a sunset over the Pacific for the first time after Lasik, you can't replicate that beauty again. I actually bite my lip and pull the bed sheet up just below my chin, that's how anxious I am.

"You ready for this?" She asked.

I meekly replied, "Yes," as if I was Peter fucking Brady and my first pube had come in.

At this point, all ego had gone out the window and I was as awestruck as a 12 year-old at Neverland Ranch for the first time after having lunch with Bubbles. She bites her lower lip right back before sliding down her panties, as if to put me at ease. Her bush was as big and beautifully maintained as the hedges in Athens, Georgia before the first kickoff of the fall. I could physically feel my boner trying to escape the end of it's skin. That's the biggest my penis has ever been. I could have taken a giraffe's temperature with this fucking thing.

As she slides into bed, raw instincts kick in and I become the generous lover I've always been known to be. She deserved it after that power point presentation, and you know *X gone give it to you.* Trying to maintain some semblance of order was virtually impossible. She moans like she's at a fucking séance trying to bring her nephew back from a wolf attack. It was just so animalistic.

So much so, all the other patients started wheeling in from other rooms. Para's, full fucking quads, even patients attached to IV's were wheelin' up to this bitch. I can see their shadows outside the closed curtain as our love-making reached epic proportions. Men share oxygen tanks and masks, crack open smelling salts—shiiiiiit one dude stroked out mid-fuck sesh and hit the floor. I can see his legs, ankle high, poking in from under the curtain. This only made me work harder. I pick up my thrusts like boosters peeling off of Apollo 13 breaking through Earth's final atmosphere. Time to take her to the moon.

I throw back the blanket entirely now and start giving her everything that's left inside of me. The crowd wanted it almost as much as I did. Part of me thought of not pulling out, but this moment was bigger than me and it would have been selfish. These people needed the ropes the Navy could not knot provide. That's a subtle, but brilliant pun. So. I. Gave. It. To. Them.

Right as she was reaching her sixth orgasm, I arched my back and pulled out. My shadow from behind the curtain must have looked like Prince playing Purple Rain during

Super Bowl XLI. Her body convulsed as I pull out my nine and unleash the rare "triple axel" of ropes. There was so much cum, a man's heart monitor went into cardiac arrest and he died immediately. I continue until every last ounce was forced out of my scrotum. Before I could exhale and admire my canvas, the curtain suddenly ripped back. Standing there, blood boiling over with anger was Sergeant Whitsaw.

"WHAT THE FUCK, BETTY?"

"Lance, what are you doing here? I'm helping a patient!" she screamed as she grabs her clothes.

"Helping him put on a sex display? I'm going to fucking kill you!" he yelled at me.

"Sir, I can explain. I was just politely boning your wife, nothing more. There was no anal. The amount of cum you see might initially seem unnatural, but I can assure it is part of my life and I have been seeking help around the globe with some of the top medical experts in the field—

"Fuck you, con! You're going to die before you even get overseas," he says as he pulls out a handgun from his holster and raises it at me.

Aaaaaaannnnnnd this is my cue to jump out the fucking window. Please don't give me the old, "Saint James Street James, you already kicked the shit out of him, why not just flex your dominance one more time?"

Not like this. I don't care how bad a motherfucker you are, if you walk in on your lady getting railed out by a man like myself and see her covered in close to a full pound of semen—it's going to give you that little extra crazy you need to take down your worst enemy. Knowing this, I hopped out the second story window like a gentleman and fall safely into a set of shrubs, before walking nude back to my barracks. If nothing else, it was a great story and made me a legend on base. This completed my first full day in the military before I entered World War II.

Chapter 13
FUCKING FRANCE MAN

Tuesday June 6th, 1944

Today starts like any other day in the military. You wake up super fucking early with a bunch of dudes and stand in line to dump out where you smell a hundred other dudes disgusting shits. If you're lucky on one of these illustrious mornings, the shit only smells half as bad, and maybe you can hear two *less* people jacking off next to you. It fucking sucks and yet again, I'm ready to get out of this bullshit at all cost. I want to enjoy my dump in a mansion again where the only thing I smell other than my own shit is a personally lit hundred-dollar bill after I've had too much escargot.

On this special day however, my particular toilet was low on water and I beached my dump. There's something so distinct about a hard stink pickle hitting dry porcelain in the AM. That sound is unmistakable. So too is the fight with the toilet handle as you pull down ten or fifteen times watching the water grappling with the weight of the turd knowing goddamn well that the tide will never reach her. Usually you have to go get a plunger, jam that brown beast down the hole, and clean out the mud from the inside of the barrel. It fucking sucks... but on this day I was saved.

Sirens suddenly blare letting us know that we were headed off to battle. Truthfully, I was relieved. This meant I definitely didn't have to worry about disposing this anus cake and I can leave it for the next poor fuck to extinguish. Good luck with that gorilla finger, boss. I'd take war any day over cleaning out a plunger.

As I made my way out of the john, men darted past me, everyone getting ready for our mission. I wasn't aware of the significance of it at the time, but for those of you who don't know your history, we were heading into Normandy. My dump wasn't the only thing hitting the beach that week.

Most people refer to it as D-Day, or that Tom Hanks movie where he spent the whole time looking for that little cunt, Matt Damon. Side note Hanx, we all wanted him to die so you could go home to your wife. Fuck that dude.

I quickly suit up and stroll out to my Mustang P-51 with the confidence of a Myrtle Beach stripper when "I'm A Slave 4 U" by Britney Spears trickles through the speakers in the club. At this point, having one whole flight under my belt, I felt great about my ability as a pilot. Totally kidding. I knew I probably wasn't coming back from this shit as I strode down the tarmac.

As I get ready to climb into the plane, I feel a tap on my shoulder. I turn and see Sergeant Whitsaw. He has a bandage on his nose and two black eyes from when I knocked him the fuck out. And even though I can't see it, I imagine his ego is pretty bruised as well after the deep dicking I gave his wife.

"Private Street James," he says in a very measured tone.

"Yes?"

"I want you to know that we're on the same team out there and I'm rooting for you," he says, swallowing back his pride.

"Thank you. And I want you to know that I would have never inserted your wife in front of you without asking for permission, or unless we were at a mutual swinger's party where the rules were set when we walked in—perhaps by a hostess or a "guide". I hate to use air quotes like that around the word *guide*, but I don't want to degrade their position or importance at an event like that. I'm getting off track—we are brothers now of the Eskimo descent and I shall see you in an igloo another time good sir."

He stands there and stares at me in confusion. "What the fuck are you talking about man?"

"I appreciate the well wishes," I say as I pat him on the shoulder.

After a few moments, he awkwardly salutes me and I return the acknowledgement. I then give that classic Saint James Street James thousand-yard stare into the horizon when I want people to get the fuck out of my face. He quickly turns and walks off as I continue to hold my gaze for another thirty to forty seconds in case he looks back. It really freaks people the fuck out and I can't recommend it enough.

Once this dick is out of sight, I climb into the cockpit and press a bunch of buttons the same way I did on the other plane. It starts up just as quickly as the last time. Holy Christ this shit is easy. You ever wonder why private jet pilots are so fucked up in real life? Rhetorical. You're probably not rich enough to do that shit like I am, but by the oft chance you are, it's because FLYING IS A GODDAMN JOKE. Literally anyone could do it. I wouldn't be surprised if someone stole a commercial airliner one day and did a fucking barrel roll in it.

We took off out of Britain and flew high over the English Channel making our way towards France. The flight was about an hour and a half, which is way too long to be on a plane without drinking. I don't care who are, everyone knows the rules of the sky—one hour plus, bottoms up son. Flying sober really isn't flying at all. You might as well walk to your destination.

I smuggled a growler of English lager onto the plane with me to get me through the mission. As I popped the top to enjoy some suds, I spot a young drunk couple fucking in the doggy style posish as I fly over Ireland. I immediately leave my formation in the sky to do a quick fly by and enjoy a quick jack sesh. A pale redhead with anything above a decent C-cup will get me every time. I'm sure the other pilots respected my decision. I turn the plane over and open up a window as I came and so it would land on her tits. Perfect execution. I bet her boyfriend appreciated it from a real American flyboy. Just a little treat from the good ole' balls of the U-S-Of-Fucking-A.

My jerk-barrel roll in under two minutes was pretty astonishing. If scientists take into consideration the difficulty and precision this took, it will pretty much make you shut the fuck up about whatever Roger Bannister[6] did. Sadly, this was the first and last time I jerked off over Ireland. It is a fond memory that I hold dear to this day though.

After finishing, I find my way back to the rear of the formation as we take aim toward France. The Instagram models who fuck old dudes so they can travel and always talk about France and "how you must go" really is true. It's the fucking best; the women, the wine, the food, the clown colleges. Plus, if you have half a sac you can literally do whatever the fuck you want because the men are such pussies over there. Chances are, if you've met a cuck in this life, I guarantee you the dude was French. He probably buried his tears deep into a beret as he sat outside the door peeking through his bedroom window. What-the-fuck-ever. We all can't be Alphas in this life. There's a reason America always saves this goddamn country, it's beauty and cuckness are unmatched. It's one of the few countries in this world I won't talk shit about.

As we flew over the coastline, our job was to wipe out the enemy so our boys could hit the beaches safely. Translation: fire as many bullets and drop as many bombs as we could until we were out and then try to make it back safely to England and reload. That proved to be a lot tougher than it

---

6   Roger Bannister was the first man to break a four-minute mile. Big. Fucking. Deal. Bro.

sounded, especially for someone with one total flight and no landing experience. Who fucking knew?

Look, I'm not going to lie to you and tell you I was the greatest pilot who ever lived, far from it. I was "a" pilot who could successfully mash buttons and keep this beautiful bitch in the air in a relatively straight line, which is exactly what I did. Nothing could prepare you though for the chaos of Normandy. There was so much firepower being hurled from every single direction it was impossible to see where it was coming from. Half of the planes in front of me were hit and began spiraling out. Billows of smoke hit my windshield and I was basically flying blind.

I knew it was inevitable that I would get hit too, so I squeezed the trigs and let the rest of my bullets fly until I had nothing left. Seconds later, I hear seven or eight bullets hit the right side of my bird. One bullet hit my right thigh, and another hit my growler causing it to shatter. Obviously, I was more pissed about my growler. There were probably three or four swigs left in it and that's something I'm going to have to live with the rest of my life. To this day, I don't know how many ounces were lost, but goddamnit if it still doesn't haunt me. If you're in the Normandy area and want to leave a growler on the beach for my lost one, just know I'm grateful to you.

I pull the plane up hard to clear the smoke and head north desperately trying to make it back to England. With blood visibly flowing through my pants, I chew a sleeve off my jacket and tie it around the wound. As soon as I tie it off, my left engine blew and the plane begins to drop. Son of a bitch. That's when I realize I don't have any morphine. Also, I probably wasn't making it to England.

It wasn't long until the right engine gave out as well. As smoke pours out of both engines now, the propellers stop completely and I knew I was fucked. My only option was to crash this bitch safely, which luckily, I had already done. Now that I think about it, they should definitely teach every pilot to do this. That way, when you actually do go down, you're not a fucking John Denver. I definitely wouldn't have learned this bullshit in basic training. Fuck you for trying to make me do that shit, slapdicks. Learn by doing.

As my plane coasts downward slowly, I notice what appears to be a horse farm just off to my left. I veer this bitch just past it, safely into the countryside. And yes, since you're wondering, I spared the horses. I value a horse more than a man any day. The other thing I value is a huge heaving set of tiddies, which are running full speed toward my plane after I take a massive divot out of the land.

I was full Dicaprio in *Aviator* with this crash. My plane was on fire and I was fucking trapped. I had no idea who the woman was running toward me with a shovel, but if I ever want to fuck her, I needed to be "not all burnt up and shit". With the fire racing toward the cockpit, she takes the shovel and bashes out the window, which allows me to pull myself out. I burn a few digits trying to escape, but at least the moneymaker and ding-dong were safe. (I know you were worried, so I soothed you.)

With my right leg almost completely numb, I hit the ground pretty hard after exiting the aircraft. The beautiful

French woman who had smashed the window in, stands over me as I drift in and out of consciousness. She was one of the hottest women I've ever seen, and I put that on my momma. Picture the chick from the movie *Amelie*, but with really huge cans. *Yeah, a pure fucking unadulterated smoke show.* She was 28 years old, but I let that part slide. In France, you want an older woman. Sexually, they were just more advanced. She looks down at me with kind eyes.

"American?" She asked in a French accent.

"We," I respond as if I had lived there for thirty years.

The French accent is strange. It's incredibly sexy on a woman, but on a man, it makes you sound like a pompous dickhole. I hate being talked to by Frenchmen, because it always sounds so goddamn condescending. That's why the first question I asked her was obviously—

"So, do you have a husband I need to beat down or—

"No. He passed in the war. It's just been me trying to fend for myself."

"I'm not sorry to hear that. The name is Saint James Street James. You?"

"Bridgette. Sorry we had to meet under these circumstances."

"I'm actually fine with it. A steed and a beautiful lady is just my jam. Also, I want you to know that I do have current feeling in my penis, so it probably works. Please don't let this gunshot to the leg make you think otherwise. I'd hate for that to be your first impression."

"It wasn't."

"I can hear you out with your girlfriends sharing a glass of chard saying 'I met this handsome, chiseled, American man who crashed into my front yard, but he has this huge limp dick.' That would break my heart."

"Please, we must get out of here quickly. This land is occupied by the Germans. Their soldiers will be here soon from the sight of your plane going down. I can assure you of this."

"I'm as concerned with the Nazis as I am about this upcoming cold and flu season I've heard about here."

She looks at me strangely. "That's a really weird thing to say."

"Well, it's a silent killer and people are fucking babies. You have a horse in those stables?"

"Yes," she replies.

"Great. Take me there. I'm having a little problem with this leg, so I'll need some assistance. Once again, my quiver bone still works."

"Yes, I heard you. Let's go."

She puts my arm around her shoulder and assists me to the stables which are three hundred yards or so away. I look down down at my leg as it drags behind me and I notice I'm losing a lot of fucking blood. This ain't no paintball wound, holmes. This is the type of shit that needs to be addressed or I might lose the whole goddamn thing. They still didn't have the proper shit back then, so I could have been amped real quick if I let this go. The bigger problem is the German military truck racing down from over the hillside. I need to get inside this barn ASAP and get back on a steed again, where I always have the advantage.

Chapter 14

AN ANIMAL BETWEEN MY LEGS

As we enter the horse stables, the smell brought back all the feels of my own. It had been close to fifty years since I've been back in one and I fucking missed it. The first thing I notice was this beautiful cleaned out trough that looked exactly like the one I used to fuck in. Maybe they're all the same. Who knows? Anywho, her horse was pretty rad too.

This steed is beautiful and reminds me of my own. His coat is a little more sleek than my old one, but let's face it Coloma, California ain't the country side of France. I limp over to the horse, lock eyes with him, and begin to run my hand down his snout. He settles down, recognizing that I ain't no bitch.

"What's his name?"

"Bisous," she replies.

"Bisous? What does that mean?"

"It means 'Kisses' in French."

"Who the fuck named him that?"

"My husband, the one I was telling you about, who is now deceased."

"Well, there's obviously a reason for that. A man doesn't name his horse 'Kisses' for Christ sakes. No wonder he's dead. How did he die, choking on his own cock?"

Bridgette takes a defensive stance and crosses her arms. "Oh yeah, what do you Americans name your horses?"

"It has nothing to do with America star tits. It has everything to do with being a fucking man, and a real goddamn man doesn't name his horse. It's just simply your steed," I say without looking at her as I enter the stall.

"Don't! He'll kick you!"

"No he won't. He knows my scent. My brethren. My dick and balls. My *dos manos*. He knows what I have between my legs and he senses the calm inside my jeans."

I now walk directly up to the horse and go snout to snout. He doesn't move, but instead leans closer. We both close our eyes and inhale deeply. With the German truck racing closer, both man and beast begin breathing as one, knowing they'll have to be in unison to kill together and protect this woman and her land. If you don't have chicken skin right now after I just described myself in the third person in that last sentence, you haven't gotten hard since 74'. We. Are. About. To. Fuck. Shit. Up.

I hop up onto the steed with ease like it was the 1800's again. No saddle. No fucking stir-ups. Man on beast. He needed to feel me and I needed to feel him. The only thing that was missing were my pistols. Unfortunately, they don't give you those back when you leave the pokey. No need though.

In order for these Nazi fucks to not come back to this farm, I needed to get violent in the most gruesome manner possible. I wasn't sure how long this war would last, but my leg needed time to heal. A few months at least. To buy myself that type of time, I need to murder them in a fashion so unbelievable, they would need to see it with their own eyes to even fathom it. This act of violence would have to serve as the ultimate warning. A warning so severe that one wouldn't even dare set foot on this farm again in fear that it might happen to them.

As my eyes scour the barn, I spot a pitchfork. Not gruesome enough. A shovel. No need, I'm not burying these fucks. Resting near a bale of hay in the corner of the barn, I spot exactly what I need. I begin to roll up my sleeves as I nod at Bridgette.

"Hand me that old reaping hook."

"You want the sickle? Oh no, you will need more than that," she insists.

I give her that old classic Saint James Street James thousand-yard stare again. "No, the sickle will do just fine."

She runs over and grabs the sickle, handing it to me, just as the German truck halts to a stop. You can hear soldiers spilling out of the back beginning to surround the barn. The

Nazis begin cocking their rifles. I motion for Bridgette to hide in the stall behind a few bales of hay.

"You stay here until the killing is over. Do not come out under any circumstances until I come back and get you. Do you understand?"

"But what if—

"There is no 'ifs'. There is only going to be *a lot* of killing. I really can't overstate that enough. No woman or child should ever see the amount of killing I'm going to do. Fuck, I might even blindfold the goddamn horse as to not scar him."

"I'll be waiting," she says as she lifts up her skirt flashing me hard beave.

Not just any beave. 1940's French countryside beave. Is there anything more glorious than that? Take a deep inhale wherever you are right now. I fucking guarantee to you can smell it, and if you're a real hombre, you can taste it too. Now it was really time to kill motherfuckers in brutal fashion.

"Come out with your hands up and we will kill you instantly instead of tying you behind the truck and dragging you down the road until you die," a man said in a thick German accent. He seemed almost bored by that statement as if he's said it many times before.

I look down at Bridgette who stares up at me in fear. "What the fuck?" I whisper.

"That's how my husband died," she whispers back.

"Then I apologize for what I said earlier. He still shouldn't have named the horse Kisses," I say with a fake tip of the cap.

"How many of you are hiding in there?" The German asks.

"It's just me. How many of you are out there?"

"Oh, you know, eighteen of your closest Nazi friends. No bigs. Let's party."

I look down at the engraving on the sickle that reads: **Revollier 18.** If this isn't fate, then you've never buttfucked raw dog inside a foam pit in Ibiza. I grab the wooden handle of the sickle tight enough to see the veins flex in my forearm.

"I'll be right out. Yee yee," I say as I squeeze the rib cage of my steed with my heels before ripping my shirt off, which is customary, and head straight for the fucking stable doors.

The horse responds exactly like my old one used to and everything came back to me in an instant as this fucker hit top speed kicking through the stable doors as if Phil Collins *In The Air Tonight* had just reached the drum section at 3 minutes and 40 seconds in. The Nazis seemed caught off guard, and I was able to slice the head off the first one who was outside the door talking shit. His dome rolls backward allowing my horse to kick it up into the air, distracting the other Nazis. I'm sure the shock of seeing your commander's head heel-kicked into the air like Pele is a bit of a surprise, which I obviously use to my advantage.

The other Nazi soldiers struggle to gain a proper grip or stance with their weapons and I was able to chop off three more of their heads with ease. I gash another Nazi violently across his chest exposing his whole fucking aortic valve. The amount of blood that sprays into my face is freakish. There was so much of it, that it didn't seem real. I pull that *Corazon* straight from his chest and smear the blood into a cross on my own chest to maximize fear. I'm not a religious man, but I am aware of the fear it strikes into other men when you're up against an enemy that thinks their vengeance is for a higher purpose.

The Nazis were scared shitless. I dart into the woods knowing they won't be able to drive their truck into that terrain. My act of madness causes them to leave the stables alone, and all of them come running toward me. I was able to see Bridgette's eyes through the slats of the wood where my steed's stall was, and I gave her the old tongue through the first two fingers indicating I was definitely going down on her later.

Yes, I am aware that I still had this dude's heart in my hand still. I know you were wondering. It only enhanced the shock for the Nazis even more, and I can see a hint of a smile from Bridgette knowing that a fucking man was finally on the property for the first time in her life. Kisses.

Once we hit the woods, I dismount my steed and hide behind a tree. The fourteen remaining Germans split up into groups of four and five, walking through the woods like a search party. I can see their faces, which look like frightened pugs. Shit, I would be too if I saw a dude lick a heart and rub that shit across his chest.

"Stay here and don't move," I instruct my steed. He nods back at me, letting me know I have established trust with all the fuckery I had just pulled off. There isn't a motherfucker alive who can talk to a horse better than me. Robert Redford can eat my dick as far as I'm concerned. Send him out to do some shit like this and tell me how his horse responds. I'm not saying I'm like Jane Goodall and those fucking monkeys but—actually, yeah, I am saying that. You can add a side of dick to Jane's order as well.

I tie my steed to a tree and quickly dive roll through the leaves behind another one about fifteen feet away. The closest group of four Germans quickly run over, rifles pointed at my horse. I left a little five-inch tall clay figurine of myself jacking off that I used to carry with me for situations like these, a top my steed. The craftsmanship was exact, which is the key element in something like this. It coerces people to come closer and examine it, then question why someone would even do something like this until—*SLIT*. I roll over and took the sickle to the back of each of their Achilles. Not just one, all four. The screams of agony were so intense, it causes the remaining nine Nazis to sprint over to our area of the woods.

I immediately hop on my steed and catch up with the first four Germans and scalped them from left to right. One of them was able to squeeze off a shot that went right through my left shoulder. Luckily, it was a clean exit, but it still stung like a motherfucker. I'm obviously ambi-dex, but now my entire left side is rendered virtually useless. With my right leg hit and my left shoulder out, I gotta finish off the remaining five soldiers relatively quick before I bleed out completely. I sure would miss that beave and it would definitely haunt me in the afterlife if I didn't get to taste it. You know I need that whisker biscuit.

I quickly survey the land and see a creek about two hundred yards down hill, so I head that way. There were two huge boulders firmly entrenched into the water, which would not only provide me shelter from their guns, but it would lend cover to my steed who could drink up, while I address my wounds. I'm slightly wishing I didn't rip my shirt off in the stable, because I could sure use those goddamn sleeves as makeshift tourniquets right about now.

As I ride closer to the water and catch a glimpse of my ripped physique covered in blood, that thought quickly fades away once I see my full dominance on display. It's just like Andre Agassi used to say when he had a full head of blonde tips and neon spandex, *image is everything*. He was goddamn right about that.

I lead my steed into the water, which is only about knee deep to him. Once we are safely behind a boulder, I jump down as well so both of us can take cover. I wasn't about to leave him in this sitch. These Nazi cocksuckers would have blown him away just to do it at this point.

The Germans were even more ruthless than your bullshit kid's history textbooks depict. The stories I heard over there were some of the most fucked up, awful, things one could ever hear in this life. Enough so, that I wasn't leaving this fucking horse to fend for his own.

With five Nazis left to kill and my steed and I behind a boulder, I knew this sickle wasn't going to cut it at this point. It's never too late for a pun like that, but this time I actually mean it. I poke my head out from behind the boulder to see their position, and immediately hear two gun shots ricochet just above my head off the top of the rock. These motherfuckers were just standing five across in the fucking stream without a care in the world. They know I don't have a gun and they roar with laughter.

The oldest of the Nazis, a big burly fucking dude in his mid 40's, lights up a cigarette as he holsters his gun. "What are you going to do now, *throw your sickle at us?*" he asks in a thick German accent.

I look down in the water and spot a handful of pebbles between my boots, grabbing them with my right hand. From their lineup, the third guy from the left is the weakest. He's pale, way too thin for his frame, and he has a loose grip on his weapon. You can tell he's used to the burly one doing all the heavy lifting when it comes to the rape and pillaging aspect, and he's definitely the last dick in at the gang bang. For these reasons, he's the motherfucker I have to *Andy Griffith.*

I peek out behind the boulder and skip three pebbles off the top of the water while I whistle. The first stone skips up and knocks out his front teeth, jamming his lit cigarette down his throat in the process. Now, the second stone was just for me. It was a pristine nut shot that definitely hit his left testicle so square that explodes on impact. He couldn't even scream due to the rock in his mouth from the first shot, instead he tries to cough it up causing his eyes to protrude from his head. The last rock I skip off his fucking forehead knocking him unconscious, sending his body floating down stream.

The Nazis scramble for their weapons, firing off what seems like endless rounds off the boulder and beneath the water around me. They didn't even think about grabbing his body, as I patiently wait for it to drift to me. As he coasts by, I grab this motherfucker by his boots and pull him toward me. The Germans still keep firing with ten or so shots killing him instantly before I can fully reel him in. One was a headshot that turns his head into a half moon crescent on his bald fade. I told you these assholes don't care, and this was one of their own. Imagine what they did in these concentration camps... or what they would do to me.

I quickly pull off the rifle that was hanging from around his neck and grab his pistol from his holster. This was all I needed. I slap the ass of my steed and give him an index finger skyward, indicating for him to rise up on his hind legs out of the water, head high above the boulder. With their gunfire hailing in, it allowed me to dip out from the opposite side of the boulder and squeeze off two more head shots. You know goddamn well I was able to grab another one and pull his pistol off of him too once he floated downstream.

With me now having two pistols, you know how fucked they are. Although they weren't the pistols I was accustomed to, the one one thing I will give the Germans is that they make decent guns. So much so, I felt confident stepping out into the stream from behind the boulder, guns a' blazing. These fuckers weren't going to jam, and they were light enough that I could finally use my left hand despite being shot.

I was patient as shit too. The game always slows down to a murderer like myself. I'm able to enjoy the moment and appreciate the kill. Call me old fashioned, but the first of the remaining three, I went with the heart shot. There's something really satisfying about seeing a man's eyes go wide for three seconds, then looking down at the wound in shock before he dies. It's like digging your hand into a bag of endless bag of Halloween candy and pulling out a miniature Snickers bar on the first try. I was feeling *Whitney* after it… especially because the big burly one was out of bullets. Whoospy ding-dong. I'm the wrong the hombre for that to happen around. I'll get to him in a moment, keep your Everclear soaked tampon in your asshole.

For the potato dick next to him, I fired off two knee shots just long enough for the sheer pain to set in, so he could hit the water and I could limp over and shoot this motherfucker right through the eye. I want the burly one to understand that I was even worse than anything he thought he was when he looked in the mirror every single morning. *Double OT. I'm the new breed. Yeah you know me.*

I kick this dude in the head as he sails by just to do it. There was so much blood downstream, you'd think this was a sorority house on their group period at Lake Havasu on the last week of Spring Break. The burly Nazi spits down into the water in front of him. He looks pissed as hell.

"Go on, get this over with American. You know I'm out of bullets!" he bristles as he holds his empty gun up.

I whistle back to my steed to come out from behind the boulder to join me by my side. Once he's within arm's length of me, I casually throw the last remaining Nazi one of my pistols. At this point, we're about fifteen feet apart. He catches it, taken aback. Instead of wildly trying to grasp it and fire off a round into my sternum, he holds the pistol and stares at me.

"What do you want me to do with this?"

"What the fuck do you think I want you to do with it? You can either jam up your ass and squeeze the trigger, or you can fight me like the man you think you are. I'm fine with either actually."

He nods slowly staring at the pistol, knowing he's outmanned. There isn't another motherfucker on this planet who would voluntarily give you his gun if he knew he wasn't far more superior than you. I also knew that the Germans had a lot of pride. One thing they can't stand is for someone to get the best of them and hold that victory over them, even in death. He pulls the gun up as fast as he possibly can—

"Fuck you," he said as he finishes his arm motion and holds the gun to his right temple.

"No. Fuck you," I say as I shoot the gun out of his hand. "For the next five seconds I want you to remember this."

He stares at me stunned as I cock my head and smile. I slowly lift my pistol, then blow his fucking brains out. The look of shock on his face right before I pull the trigger was better than that threesome in Tucson with those contortionists I was talking about in the last book. Killing a dude is the best feeling on this planet, but it's magnified by a zillion when they see you do it and there's nothing they can do about it. You flat out bested them. It's more than a victory, it's taking someone's soul in front them so quickly they can see it leave just before it escapes their body. Fuck. Him.

As this barrel chested fuck's body splashes into the water, I turn and hop on my steed and ride out. The last image of his head exploding was all that I needed. No reason to look back and admire my handy work. I still had a beaver to slay back on the farm. Goddamn. Saint James Street James hadn't lost a step. Yeah, I thought I'd go ahead and read your inner monologue to you to make it an *outer monologue*. You're welcome.

The look of excitement on Bridgette's face as I stride up over the top of the hill shirtless and bleeding was all I needed to see. You know that look you get from a recently single or divorced woman when you save their life and chances are they were dating or married to some fucking simp for years and years? *That's* the fucking vibe I was catching. I was about to get it in son, and this was going to feel greater than the first bite of a Bomb Pop to a toothless homeless man on a hot summer day. Despite my extreme blood loss, I could still feel that bad moon rising in my jeans. It was like a spiked bat fighting a *pinata*. That's how hot this girl was, that the rest of the blood inside of me went straight to my dick.

As I dismount my steed next to her, I fake "going down" as if I was almost dead. I really wanted to sell the whole "I put my life on the line for you, I'm a fucking hero" bit, which let's face it, is warranted. Before you get your pierced labia hung up in your fishnets, I earned this shit. *Nay, I deserved this shit.* I just killed a buttfuck of Nazi's, daddy deserves the spoils… and spoiled I was.

"Are you okay? There was so many of them, I was worried you wouldn't return," she says exasperated.

"I didn't have a choice. If they got past me, you would have been raped and killed… *and then probably raped again.* I couldn't live with myself if that happened. You're the most beautiful woman I've ever seen in all my travels, so it was my pleasure to crash into your farm and kill eighteen Nazis with mostly a sickle. Here is your steed back. If I could trouble you for a band aid or two that would be swell and I'll be on my way. From my plane, it looked like there was a town about 7 or 8 miles from here. I can just walk it and leave you by your lonesome—

"Oh no, no, no. You can't. You're bleeding so much. Someone needs to address these wounds immediately. Also, it would be nice to have a man around the house again in case the Germans come back. Not only was my husband killed, but my neighbors in the nearby surrounding farms were executed as well. You are all I have."

"Well, I guess I can stay for a little while, but only until I heal properly. I hate to be a burden to someone like you. God knows you're probably the object of desire for the entire town. Where as I'm just your average American hero walking around with this big ole' dumb dick, looking for a place to wash someone else's blood off my six pack abs."

"You're no burden," she says seductively. "Truthfully, you're the first attractive man I've met since my husband, and even he was—

"Less than?" I ask making the "less than" sign with my hands just in case she was a fucking dummy at math.

She shakes her head slowly. "Yes."

Her eyes well up with tears as she looks at me with hopeless desperation. I can feel her passion is genuine... *and so is my rock hard boner.* With me being fresh out of prison, shot the fuck up, and no desire to fight in another War—this is exactly what I wanted in my life at this moment. I needed her as much as she needed me, and you're Fucking A' right I was thinking about "finishing the attic"[7] with her every night. I grab her face and kiss her with the same exact same passion I had before I left for the fight. This way she knows that's what she's getting every single time.

"Let me take you into the house and fix you up. I was a nurse for the first few years of the War."

---

7 "Finishing the attic" is the code for prolonged boning. You know how an attic is going to take years to build by yourself, but you're willing to make the commitment for the resale value in a few years? This was worth it.

I look up at her beautiful house, and then down at my bleeding leg, knowing better. She doesn't want to be mopping blood out of this bitch. Plus, my steed needs a little something for the effort, you know? He probably hadn't seen them TIGS, so it was time to reward him for his bravery as well. This motherfucker hid behind a boulder with me hoping my shit was up to snuff enough to fend off a hundred rounds of bullets ricocheting around him.

"I don't want to drag blood through *our* home," I say with the warmness of a brick oven pizza. "You would just have to clean it, and there's more important things that you could be doing with your time," I say as I grab her hand and place it on my dong.

"Oh my, the—

"Girth. I know. You'll get used to it. They all do. How about you wash me up in barn? I'll trough up while you go get thirty-eight or so buckets of warm water."

"Okay, I'll grab some medical supplies as well."

"Also, take this," I say as I reach down and pick up a wooden rake, unscrewing the top. I toss the top and hand her just the wooden pole.

"What's this for?" She asks, puzzled.

"It's for the buckets of water. You pop that up on your shoulders so you can get maybe four or five buckets going at the same time depending on your glute strength. It's not all in your traps like most people think. I'm looking at those hind quarters right now, and you might be able to squeeze six across."

"Oh, I definitely can. You take your pants off and relax. I'll be back in six and half trips," she says seductively.

Turns out she was no dummy at math and I was no stranger to a goddamn barn. I drag the horse trough over to where my steed was resting and put that bitch front and center so he could enjoy the show. Due to my gunshots, it took me longer than Stephen Hawking to get my pants off, but I was finally able to safely hop inside. I look down at my leg where the bullet was lodged and grimace, this shit hurt wheel fucking bad. Yeah, I was in that much pain that I dipped into a Chinese accent on the word "real".

Moments later, my sweet Frenchess duck-walks in with the first six buckets of warm water, dumping them into the trough. I close my eyes as the hot water runs across my wounds. It was a mixture of pain and relief. The reason for the pain was obvious. The relief was in the sense that it felt nice to be back in a warm bath again and not some group shower where you're constantly watching your b-hole at every turn. I was able to relax, knowing that if a knuckle went into my dooker, it was heightening a sexual climax—not being forced into you by another man to make sure you gave him your soup tomorrow at chow hall. She pulls out a washcloth, dips it into the water, and places it on my forehead as I lean back in the trough.

"I'll be back in fifteen. Take deep breaths and try to relax," she said.

"I—

Lights out. Guerilla Radio. I was fucking out faster than Paul Lynne could say, "Hello!" I'm not even sure for how long. The next time I came to, Bridgette was in the trough with me, buck naked, riding me slowly. She had a pair of tweezers between her teeth. I looked over at my left shoulder, which was freshly wrapped. On the floor in a bowl I could see a bloody bullet removed and an empty syringe of morphine. This is the moment Saint James Street James found his second wife. You morph me up without a verbal confirmation, instead just knowing that's exactly what I need with a goddamn body like this? Congrats, we're getting married. Speaking of which—

Her body deserves its own paragraph. First off, she was cautious enough not to get her hair and face wet. From the effort she made earlier, you know she wasn't afraid to get dirty, but she wanted to keep her makeup and hair in place to let you know that she could be a *real woman* too. Not someone you would see on a thumbnail for "facial destruction" on Pornhub with mascara running down her face faster than her father ran out on her as a kid. She had curves, but wasn't a PAWG[8]. Her skin was Mediterranean, very olive, almost Italian looking.

You know dem tiddies needed a separate paragraph as well. These beagle ears were ABSOLUTE HANGERS. You could have put a Cessna 172 under each one and no one have known. The nipples were a darker shade of red, veering toward a deep maroon. Type in "100D dash 7 paint" on Home Depot's website if you're looking for a color swatch on these

---

8   PAWG stands for "phat ass white girl" you dumbshits.

dawgs. The visual is worth it. The surrounding surface around the nipples was as bumpy as Ray Charles sheet music. You know I love the braille nips.

Her ass was every bit as expected for a woman capable of carrying thirty-six buckets of warm water down hill from a country side house. The bush I described from earlier had already grown a quarter inch. If it were possible to be more in love at this point, Cupid would have put his whole dick in my mouth. This woman was better than a two-dollar egg sandwich at *The Masters*. Even all drugged up I knew she was the one.

"Are you ready?" She asks.

"For me to give you that Indiana clown pie?"

"Is that what you call 'cum' in America?"

"Gonna be honest, I've never heard it in my life. My words are just kind of glued together in a stream of semi-consciousness right now. I'm fucking flying—

"Ssssshhhh," she said as she put her finger to my lips. "Yes, shoot for me in three, two, one—

As I arch my back and unleash what feels like endless ropes inside of her, she pulls the tweezers from between her teeth and jams them into my thigh pulling the last remaining bullet out of my leg. Blood squirts up on her tits as I continue to cum, triggering her as well. The fucking steed got so charged up, he jumped out of the fucking window of the barn. This was the most surreal, intense orgasm I had ever had in my life. When a horse jumps out of a goddamn window, you know shit was live.

I awoke in a strange bed the following morning in a house that smelled like home. A fresh flower was laying on the pillow next to me with a crutch resting up against the bed. As I gingerly make my way down the stairs, I see Bridgette in the kitchen topless, making pancakes. It was as priceless as you can imagine. After breakfast, we shared a screw followed by a carafe of orange juice and a bottle of champers.

This was as close to perfect as it's ever been for me in my life, which is hard to admit. Hindsight is looking at your own asshole in a full length mirror through your legs, but if I'm honest with myself, this is when I was the happiest. I was completely at peace and I wasn't going to let anything ruin it... so I did the only thing a man can do to keep motherfuckers off my property. As I get up out of bed, Bridgette squeezes my bicep.

"Where are you going?" She axed.

"I'm going to take care of those bodies before anyone else finds them. If any Nazi's see that bloodbath, they'll be looking for the man who did this."

"But your leg—

"The third one? I know. This boner will eventually subside. In the meantime, I'm going to get dressed and take that steed out around the property to clean up. Do you have any diesel gasoline by any chance?"

"Of course, it's in the garage. I used to huff on it out of boredom but you're welcome to use it. Can I ask what you're going to do with it?"

"Sure. It rhymes with 'German Bonfire,'" I say as I mime flames with my fingers like Jimi Hendrix on stage at the Monterey Pop Fest.

She nods her head slowly without looking up at me then, "Okay. I'll make some coffee. Torch those assholes."

"Goddamn right I will," I say slightly amused. "I'll make sure no one ever steps foot on this property again."

I kiss her forehead and begin to slide on my jeans as I watch her sweet ass saunter down the stairs buck naked. She was so confident in her body that she didn't even bother attempting to cover up. Bridgette knew the assets she had, flaunted it, and made damn sure I knew what I was coming home to at night. There's nothing sexier in the world than that and it made me feel lucky that I was the one fucking her.

"My ass isn't the only thing that's choice around here, I also make great coffee," she calls out over her shoulder.

Motherfucker. She knew what I was thinking. Later on, as I walk out to the barn sipping the coffee, she was right. This is the best cup of joe I've had in my entire life. The only way I'd be more surprised now is if I came home and she had a mute identical twin. Let's face it, I don't want two women talking in the house at the same time.

For the next three or four hours, I tie dead German soldiers to the back of my steed and drag them into a makeshift pile next to a large tree stump. One by one I remove their pants and lay them across the stump. With a large axe I retrieved from the barn, I chop the dick and balls off of every

Nazi, before discarding their bodies into a flesh pyramid. When I was done and had them stacked properly, I set them ablaze with the diesel gasoline Bridgette used to huff on from the garage.

The smell of the burning flesh was horrific, yet somehow cathartic. It was like quitting smoking for a week and your drunk Aunt comes in from the back porch after puffing on a Capri 120 Thanksgiving night after the pecan pie was served. You know that stink, and you're surprised you used to enjoy it.

With the bodies emitting plumes of smoke toward the sky, I pull out a clothesline I had taken from the backyard, and wet the line with my tongue while whistling a show tune from a Jewish composer. It was only fitting. I kept whistling as I slid the wet line through a large sewing needle. Once the line was taught, I pierce the needle through each set of dick and balls, which I had removed, and string them out like serial killer Christmas ornaments. One ball, one dick, repeat. It was quite a sight if you could stomach it. Most men couldn't, which is why I strung them up above the property line hung between the two trees that bookend the front gate.

There was an old faded wooden sign that read, "Lefrebre Manor." I removed that bullshit, pulled out my buck knife that was strapped to my calf and whittled in, **"St. James Place, Bitch. Enter and I'll Cut Your Fucking Dick Off Too. Look Up If You Don't Believe Me."** It took every ounce inside of me to keep it so subtle, but I somehow managed it. I was proud of myself.

Needless to say, word spread throughout town, and no one dared to step foot on our land until the war ended. I was so content here, I didn't even read a newspaper, probably because I didn't speak the language, but also I just didn't care. Home girl had money, and I really didn't have to do anything except tend to the farm, ride my steed, and have sex all day. Even when I found out the war had ended, I didn't even make an attempt to leave. I had no reason to return to America at this point, and there was not one single thing I needed to go back for. Out here, I was completely free of all worry and responsibility.

I drank the best wine, had unimaginable sex every day, and was fed like a fucking king. She made me laugh endlessly and challenged me mentally. This was my Johnny Depp phase when he was cool and mysterious, before he became a caricature of himself. I lived in France for the next fourteen years with Bridgette on that farm, and I can promise you that she'll be one of the last people that goes through my mind before I pull the trigger at the end of these memoirs... *it just isn't going to be right now though.*

I'm getting closer and closer with each stroke on the typewriter, I can assure you that. However, this isn't the way to end it. After years of turmoil, I'm going to light a heater and reminisce over the good times, brother. Most men do at the end of their life.

You'll realize it when you get toward the end like I am today in 2015. There are one or two women over the course of your life that you won't be able to shake no matter how hard you try. Hell, part of you doesn't want to either. You'll always have regrets, that's natural. It's realizing how valuable time is.

You can't go back in time, and can't buy more of it, no matter how rich you are. I guess you could cut your fucking head off and stick it in a freezer like Walt Disney, but you'll be using someone else's cock when you get back *hombre*—and that ain't no way to live. So instead, I'm going to enjoy this smoke like I was laying in bed with that French chick again post coital for the thousandth time, without a care in the world… because the rest of my life is a goddamn beautiful disaster. You'll see in the next book, fuckfaces.

CPSIA information can be obtained
at www.ICGtesting.com
Printed in the USA
LVHW031541011220
673096LV00040B/681/J